JOHN DRYDEN
Poems selected by
CHARLES TOMLINSON

faber and faber

First published in 2004
by Faber and Faber Limited
3 Queen Square London WC1N 3AU

Photoset by Wilmaset Ltd, Birkenhead, Wirral
Printed in England by Bookmarque Ltd, Croydon

A CIP record for this book
is available from the British Library

ISBN 0–571–21478–9

10 9 8 7 6 5 4 3 2 1

THE LONDON BOROUGH

ORPINGTON LIBRARY
01689 831551

Please return this item by the last date stamped below, to the librar
it was borrowed.

Renewals
Any item may be renewed twice by telephone or post, provided it i
required by another customer. Please quote the barcode number.

Overdue Charges
Please see library notices for the current rate of charges levied on
items. Please note that the overdue charges are made on junior bo
on adult tickets.

Postage
Postage on overdue notices is payable.

1 2 NOV 2007		
- 3 APR 2020		
	W D	

To Brenda

Contents

Introduction

John Dryden (1631–1700) is the kind of writer much valued by other poets. Coleridge, Tennyson, Hopkins, Eliot all express their admiration. The first major figure to do this was Alexander Pope in his *Essay on Criticism*. The central force that Dryden brought to his public was the intellectual energy that pervades the movement of his verse. As Pope writes,

> Waller was smooth, but Dryden taught to join
> The varying verse, the full-resounding line,
> The long majestick march and energy divine.

The energy manifests itself in various ways. It can enforce a massive and ungainsayable sweep of the verse, but it can be equally ungainsayable by its sheer compactness, as in the characterisation of Zimri in *Absalom and Achitophel*:

> Stiff in opinions, always in the wrong;
> Was every thing by starts and nothing long.

The snap of the trap in that gives place to a list where the helter skelter of rhythm expresses both a comic absurdity and a sort of imaginative wonder that all this could actually be so and within a single individual:

> Was Chymist, Fiddler, Statesman and Buffoon:
> Then all for Women, Painting, Rhiming, Drinking,
> Besides ten thousand freaks that dy'd in thinking.

Such effects are contained by a context which itself often has a sense of the vast and uncontrollable – a country in near chaos as in *Absalom and Achitophel*.

I first came across Dryden and his follower Pope in the years between the 1940s and 50s when English poetry often seemed to be losing its ability to handle a variety of tones. This was the period of the New Apocalypse and of all that the muddled life of Dylan Thomas seemed to sanction in terms of both style and living. For a young poet it was necessary to struggle to rediscover an idiom where one could simply say what one meant. The Augustans, with Dryden in their forefront, were a welcome antidote. So was the mutual aid between myself and Donald Davie as we criticised each other's verse. His own *Purity of Diction in English Poetry* and *Articulate Energy* (a study of poetic syntax) gave me much to think about in relation to late seventeenth-century and eighteenth-century verse. His anthology, *The Late Augustans*, marked both our steps as we moved from Dryden to the age of Cowper and talked over our latest discoveries. But at the back of it all loomed the example of Dryden himself – what was 'articulate energy' but the 'energy divine' that Pope attributes to him?

Dr Johnson quotes Pope's line in his life of the poet and adds to it a commendation of his own: 'His compositions are the effects of a vigorous genius operating upon large materials.' Johnson's description grows in accuracy once Dryden begins to focus on aims that had been dissipated by years of writing for the Restoration stage. Unlike his contemporary, Milton, Dryden could rely on no paternal wealth to support him in producing a single great work. He said of his own theatrical ventures, 'I knew that they were bad enough to please even when I wrote them.' Though, even in these works, passages stand out from the general run of things, like the pessimistic one in the heroic play *Aureng-Zebe* that opens

> When I consider Life, 'tis all a cheat;
> Yet fool'd with hope, men favour the deceit.

The fanciful description of night in *The Indian Emperour* –

> The little Birds in Dreams their Songs repeat,
> And sleeping flowers beneath the night-dew sweat

– stayed long in the minds of eighteenth-century readers, long enough to be recalled in her journal by Johnson's friend, Mrs Piozzi, and placed close to Shakespeare.

The great popularity of *Annus Mirabilis: the Year of Wonders*

(1666), a sort of mini-epic on recent English history and a poem full of lively if extravagant conceits, was a factor in Dryden's obtaining the poet laureateship and the post of historiographer royal two years later, at the age of thirty-seven. These lasted until he became a Catholic in the late 1680s and the exile of our last Catholic monarch and the arrival of William of Orange. He was to achieve the satiric verve of *Absalom and Achitophel* (1681) only in his fifties. It was once customary to see this poem, along with *Mac Flecknoe* (1676 and 1684) – the work Pope variated and expanded on in *The Dunciad* – as evidence that Dryden was chiefly a satiric poet, though this aspect of his verse merely occupies a small portion of his collected works.

In excerpting *Absalom and Achitophel*, I have drawn chiefly on the varied characters in this allegory based on the turmoils of King David's reign in biblical times. The English become the Jews, Charles II is David and the Earl of Shaftesbury Achitophel, who backs Absalom (Charles's illegitimate son, the Duke of Monmouth) for the succession against Charles's brother, James, who was a Catholic. But the shock of recognition in all this cannot quite affect us with the force that it did Dryden's first readers. What does is his characterisation of human types in their wide variety. Of the structure of the poem as a whole and the allegorical form in particular, Johnson comments: 'Allegories drawn to great length will always break. Charles could not run continually parallel with David.' All the same, Dryden's panorama of his times sets him head and shoulders above his contemporaries with that unparalleled sense of 'a vigorous genius operating upon large materials'.

The same chaotic divisions as in *Absalom and Achitophel*, together with religious sectarianism, resulted in *Religio Laici, or A Laymans Faith* (1682), which makes the case for the steadying presence of the Church of England. This was the kind of work that set the later nineteenth century against Dryden – a discussion in verse, it was felt, could hardly be a poem. Matthew Arnold, taking Dryden and Pope as the principal malefactors, tells us that 'their poetry is conceived in the wits, genuine poetry is conceived and composed in the soul'. What he meant by the soul seems to be the mood of self-indulgent pastoralism that inspired his own 'Scholar Gypsy'. Though the Victorian age had definitely cooled towards Dryden, there were exceptions. One of the most intelligent was Gerard Manley Hopkins, for whom Dryden's language was not, as others maintained, 'prosaic', but vivid and alive. Defending Dryden against Robert Bridges, Hopkins insisted: 'He is the most masculine of our poets; his style and rhythms lay the strongest stress of all our literature on the naked thew and sinew of the English language.'

Earlier in the century, Sir Walter Scott, a considerable poet in his own right (though now out of favour), had been Dryden's most judicious editor. North of the border once more, in 1845 *Blackwood's Edinburgh Magazine* printed a series of essays on Dryden that have never been surpassed. Their author was Christopher North, alias John Wilson, an admirer and friend of Wordsworth. They contained the first extended criticism of Dryden's great translations of Virgil and of Chaucer (these are now available in a Scholars' Facsimiles and Reprints edition).

One other poem of length appeared before the full range of Dryden's powers as a translator displayed themselves. This was *The Hind and the Panther* (1687), a defence of the Roman Church, which must have doomed his reputation further with the Victorians. *The Hind and the Panther* uses arguments on reason and faith which are identical with those in *Religio Laici*, where the Anglican Church had been his hope for England and its sectarian divisions. As a Catholic Dryden espoused moderation, but he continued to speak out against both the priesthood and the Jesuits. The poem uses a beast fable (hence its title) to take some of the acrimony out of the discussion. This is a form modern readers find difficult to accept and Johnson himself had his reservations about it, commenting, 'What can be more absurd than that one beast should counsel another to rest her faith upon a pope and council.'

Dryden's religion finally cost him his laureateship, which was given to his old enemy, the poet Thomas Shadwell (lampooned in *Mac Flecknoe*). And as he ruefully tells Congreve, the man he looked on as his true successor, 'Tom the Second reigns like Tom the First.' Ultimate submission to church authority remains in character with the younger Dryden, who had counted on the authority of a Cromwell to pacify and unify the country and in whose government office he had worked beside Marvell and Milton. One of his earliest poems is an ode on the death of the Great Protector.

A personal crisis, arising out of a feeling of having wasted his powers and helped 'T'increase the steaming ordures of the stage', changes the nature of Dryden's work. Once we arrive at *Sylvae* (1685) we see his emergence in his mid-fifties as the finest poet-translator of his time and of succeeding times, an aspect I have sought to represent fully in this selection. The kind of translation Dryden came to prefer was, as he said, 'paraphrase, or translation with latitude, where the author is kept in view by the translator so as never to be lost, but his words are not so strictly followed as his sense, and that too is admitted to be amplified, but not altered'. He avoids the word-by-word and line-by-line approach, or what he calls 'metaphrase'. He distrusts 'imitation', or adaptation as we should say. Nevertheless he found it hard in practice to steer clear of 'adapting' and later confesses, 'I have both added and omitted.' Thus, a connoisseur of metamorphosis in his translations of Ovid, Dryden is always discovering shared elements between his translated authors, coincidences of thought and feeling. The translations reach out to one another across the centuries as he moves from Virgil to Chaucer and Boccaccio. Although Dryden wrote no single great work like Milton's *Paradise Lost*, the recurrences of themes and even of turns of phrase give a pattern to his many translations, thus affording an experience of unity. Finding a voice for Lucretius and Horace extends his own range as a poet, and his version of Virgil's *Aeneid* (1697) creates one of the narrative masterpieces of the later seventeenth century. It both challenged and encouraged the young Alexander Pope to undertake his version of Homer's *Iliad*. My own opinion is that the phase of the translations contains Dryden's very greatest and most varied work, a unique phenomenon among our poets. Who else has produced a body of poetry in any way comparable except possibly Ezra Pound?

Dryden's final volume, *Fables Ancient and Modern* (1700), contained a number of translated narrative poems from the past from Ancient Greece and Rome, medieval England and Italy. These 'made it new' (in Pound's phrase) especially for poets themselves. From the comments of Scott, Wordsworth, Byron, Keats and Tennyson, these translations evidently seemed to them as fresh as the day they were penned. The same is true of Pope before this later generation. Writing of Dryden's *Fables*, he declares: 'those scribblers who attacked him in his latter times were only like gnats in a summer evening, which are never very troublesome but in the finest and most glorious season; for his fire, like the sun's, shined clearest towards his setting.' For too long, Dryden was looked on merely as a satirist and controversialist (which he magnificently was), but the fire of which Pope speaks was that of a great poet, the measure of whose greatness can only be taken if we see him as a great translator too.

Johnson in his *Lives of the English Poets* still remains Dryden's greatest critic. The most helpful modern work I have come across is *John Dryden* (1986) by David Hopkins. Robin Sowerby's selection, *Dryden's Aeneid* (1986), is prefaced by an exceptional introduction.

CHARLES TOMLINSON

Textual Note

The texts printed here are taken from the most easily come by edition, *The Poems of John Dryden* (1958) edited by James Kinsley, in four volumes. The dates of Dryden's various books are given in my introduction. The selection of his many translations appears in the chronological order of the original authors. I have placed square brackets round my own titles of extracts.

C.T.

JOHN DRYDEN

from Annus Mirabilis: the Year of Wonders, 1666

[The Fire of London]

Such was the rise of this prodigious fire,
  Which in mean buildings first obscurely bred,
From thence did soon to open streets aspire,
  And straight to Palaces and Temples spread.

The diligence of Trades and noiseful gain,
  And luxury, more late, asleep were laid:
All was the nights, and in her silent reign,
  No sound the rest of Nature did invade.

In this deep quiet, from what source unknown,
  Those seeds of fire their fatal birth disclose:
And first, few scatt'ring sparks about were blown,
  Big with the flames that to our ruine rose.

Then, in some close-pent room it crept along,
  And, smouldring as it went, in silence fed:
Till th' infant monster, with devouring strong,
  Walk'd boldly upright with exalted head.

Now, like some rich or mighty Murderer,
  Too great for prison, which he breaks with gold:
Who fresher for new mischiefs does appear,
  And dares the world to tax him with the old:

So scapes th' insulting fire his narrow Jail,
  And makes small out-lets into open air:
There the fierce winds his tender force assail,
  And beat him down-ward to his first repair.

The winds, like crafty Courtezans, with-held
  His flames from burning, but to blow them more:
And, every fresh attempt, he is repell'd
  With faint denials, weaker then before.

3

And now, no longer letted of his prey,
    He leaps up at it with inrag'd desire:
O'r-looks the neighbours with a wide survey,
    And nods at every house his threatning fire.

[The Dutch at Bergen]

And now approach'd their Fleet from *India*, fraught
    With all the riches of the rising Sun:
And precious Sand from Southern Climates brought,
    (The fatal Regions where the War begun.)

Like hunted *Castors*, conscious of their store,
    Their way-laid wealth to *Norway*'s coasts they bring:
There first the North's cold bosome Spices bore,
    And Winter brooded on the Eastern Spring.

By the rich scent we found our perfum'd prey,
    Which flanck'd with Rocks did close in covert lie:
And round about their murdering Canon lay,
    At once to threaten and invite the eye.

Fiercer then Canon, and then Rocks more hard,
    The *English* undertake th' unequal War:
Seven Ships alone, by which the Port is barr'd,
    Besiege the *Indies*, and all *Denmark* dare.

These fight like Husbands, but like Lovers those:
    These fain would keep, and those more fain enjoy:
And to such height their frantick passion grows,
    That what both love, both hazard to destroy.

Amidst whole heaps of Spices lights a Ball,
    And now their Odours arm'd against them flie:
Some preciously by shatter'd Porc'lain fall,
    And some by Aromatick splinters die.

from Absalom and Achitophel

[King David]*

In pious times, e'r Priest-craft did begin,
Before *Polygamy* was made a sin;
When man, on many, multiply'd his kind,
E'r one to one was, cursedly, confind:
When Nature prompted, and no law deny'd
Promiscuous use of Concubine and Bride;
Then, *Israel*'s Monarch, after Heaven's own heart,
His vigorous warmth did, variously, impart
To Wives and Slaves: And, wide as his Command,
Scatter'd his Maker's Image through the Land.
Michal, of Royal blood, the Crown did wear,
A Soyl ungratefull to the Tiller's care:
Not so the rest; for several Mothers bore
To Godlike *David*, several Sons before.
But since like slaves his bed they did ascend,
No True Succession could their seed attend.
Of all this Numerous Progeny was none
So Beautifull, so brave, as *Absalom*;
Whether, inspir'd by some diviner Lust,
His Father got him with a greater Gust;
Or that his Conscious destiny made way
By manly beauty to Imperiall sway.
Early in Foreign fields he won Renown,
With Kings and States ally'd to *Israel*'s Crown:
In Peace the thoughts of War he could remove,
And seem'd as he were only born for love.
What e'r he did was done with so much ease,
In him alone, 'twas Natural to please.
His motions all accompanied with grace;

* Charles II

And *Paradise* was open'd in his face.
With secret Joy, indulgent *David* view'd
His Youthfull Image in his Son renew'd ...
What faults he had (for who from faults is free?)
His Father could not, or he would not see.
Some warm excesses, which the Law forbore,
Were constru'd Youth that purg'd by boyling o'r ...

[The Jews]*

The *Jews*, a Headstrong, Moody, Murmuring race,
As ever try'd th' extent and stretch of grace;
God's pamper'd people whom, debauch'd with ease,
No King could govern, nor no God could please;
(Gods they had tri'd of every shape and size
That God-smiths could produce, or Priests devise:)
These *Adam*-wits, too fortunately free,
Began to dream they wanted libertie;
And when no rule, no president was found
Of men, by Laws less circumscrib'd and bound,
They led their wild desires to Woods and Caves,
And thought that all but Savages were Slaves.

[Achitophel]†

Some by their Monarch's fatal mercy grown,
From Pardon'd Rebels, Kinsmen to the Throne;
Were rais'd in Power and publick Office high:
Strong Bands, if Bands ungratefull men could tye.
  Of these the false *Achitophel* was first:
A Name to all succeeding Ages Curst.
For close Designs, and crooked Counsels fit;
Sagacious, Bold, and Turbulent of wit:
Restless, unfixt in Principles and Place;

* The English
† The Earl of Shaftesbury

6

In Power unpleas'd, impatient of Disgrace.
A fiery Soul, which working out its way,
Fretted the Pigmy Body to decay:
And o'r inform'd the Tenement of Clay.
A daring Pilot in extremity;
Pleas'd with the Danger, when the Waves went high
He sought the Storms; but for a Calm unfit,
Would Steer too nigh the Sands, to boast his Wit.
Great Wits are sure to Madness near ally'd;
And thin Partitions do their Bounds divide:
Else, why should he, with Wealth and Honour blest,
Refuse his Age the needful hours of Rest?
Punish a Body which he coud not please;
Bankrupt of Life, yet Prodigal of Ease?
And all to leave, what with his Toyl he won,
To that unfeather'd, two Leg'd thing, a Son:
Got, while his Soul did hudled Notions try;
And born a shapeless Lump, like Anarchy.
In Friendship False, Implacable in Hate:
Resolv'd to Ruine or to Rule the State.

[Zimri]*

Some of their Chiefs were Princes of the Land:
In the first Rank of these did *Zimri* stand:
A man so various, that he seem'd to be
Not one, but all Mankinds Epitome.
Stiff in Opinions, always in the wrong;
Was every thing by starts, and nothing long:
But, in the course of one revolving Moon,
Was Chymist, Fidler, States-Man, and Buffoon:
Then all for Women, Painting, Rhiming, Drinking;
Besides ten thousand freaks that dy'd in thinking.
Blest Madman, who coud every hour employ,

* Shaftesbury's associate, the Duke of Buckingham

With something New to wish, or to enjoy!
Rayling and praising were his usual Theams;
And both (to shew his Judgment) in Extreams:
So over Violent, or over Civil,
That every man, with him, was God or Devil.
In squandring Wealth was his peculiar Art:
Nothing went unrewarded, but Desert.
Begger'd by Fools, whom still he found too late:
He had his Jest, and they had his Estate.
He laught himself from Court, then sought Relief
By forming Parties, but coud ne're be Chief:
For, spight of him, the weight of Business fell
On *Absalom* and wise *Achitophel*:
Thus, wicked but in will, of means bereft,
He left not Faction, but of that was left.

   [Shimei]*

The wretch, who Heavens Annointed dar'd to Curse.
Shimei, whose Youth did early Promise bring
Of Zeal to God, and Hatred to his King;
Did wisely from Expensive Sins refrain,
And never broke the Sabbath, but for Gain:
Nor ever was he known an Oath to vent,
Or Curse unless against the Government.
Thus, heaping Wealth, by the most ready way
Among the *Jews*, which was to Cheat and Pray;
The City, to reward his pious Hate
Against his Master, chose him Magistrate:
His Hand a Vare of Justice did uphold;
His Neck was loaded with a Chain of Gold.
During his Office, Treason was no Crime.
The sons of *Belial* had a glorious Time:
For *Shimei*, though not prodigal of pelf,

* Bethel, Sheriff of London

Yet lov'd his wicked Neighbour as himself:
When two or three were gather'd to declaim
Against the Monarch of *Jerusalem*,
Shimei was always in the midst of them.
And, if they Curst the King when he was by,
Woud rather Curse, than break good Company.
If any durst his Factious Friends accuse,
He pact a Jury of dissenting *Jews*:
Whose fellow-feeling, in the godly Cause,
Would free the suffring Saint from Humane Laws.
For Laws are only made to Punish those,
Who serve the King, and to protect his Foes.
If any leisure time he had from Power,
(Because 'tis Sin to misimploy an hour;)
His business was, by Writing, to Persuade,
That Kings were Useless, and a Clog to Trade:

[Corah]*

Yet, *Corah*, thou shalt from Oblivion pass;
Erect thy self thou Monumental Brass:
High as the Serpent of thy mettall made,
While Nations stand secure beneath thy shade.
What tho his Birth were base, yet Comets rise
From Earthy Vapours ere they shine in Skies.
Prodigious Actions may as well be done
By Weavers issue, as by Princes Son.
This Arch-Attestor for the Publick Good,
By that one Deed Enobles all his Bloud.
Who ever ask'd the Witnesses high race,
Whose Oath with Martyrdom did *Stephen* grace?
Ours was a *Levite*, and as times went then,
His Tribe were Godalmightys Gentlemen.
Sunk were his Eyes, his Voyce was harsh and loud,
Sure signs he neither Cholerick was, nor Proud:
His long Chin prov'd his Wit; his Saintlike Grace
A Church Vermilion, and a *Moses*'s Face;
His Memory, miraculously great,
Could Plots, exceeding mans belief, repeat;
Which, therefore cannot be accounted Lies,
For humane Wit could never such devise.
Some future Truths are mingled in his Book;
But, where the witness faild, the Prophet Spoke:
Some things like Visionary flights appear;
The Spirit caught him up, the Lord knows where:
And gave him his *Rabinical* degree
Unknown to Foreign University.
His Judgment yet his Memory did excel;
Which peic'd his wondrous Evidence so well ...

* Titus Oates

from The Second Part of Absalom and Achitophel

  [Og]*

  Now stop your noses Readers, all and some,
For here's a tun of Midnight-work to come,
Og from a Treason Tavern rowling home.
Round as a Globe, and Liquor'd ev'ry chink,
Goodly and Great he Sayls behind his Link;
With all this Bulk there's nothing lost in *Og*
For ev'ry inch that is not Fool is Rogue:
A Monstrous mass of foul corrupted matter,
As all the Devils had spew'd to make the batter.
When wine has given him courage to Blaspheme,
He Curses God, but God before Curst him;
And if man cou'd have reason none has more,
That made his Paunch so rich and him so poor.
With wealth he was not trusted, for Heav'n knew
What 'twas of Old to pamper up a *Jew*;
To what wou'd he on Quail and Pheasant swell,
That ev'n on Tripe and Carrion cou'd rebell?
But though Heav'n made him poor, (with rev'rence speaking,)
He never was a Poet of God's making;
The Midwife laid her hand on his Thick Skull,
With this Prophetick blessing – *Be thou Dull* ...

* Thomas Shadwell, poet

Songs

'Why Should a Foolish Marriage Vow'

Why should a foolish Marriage Vow
    Which long ago was made,
Oblige us to each other now
    When Passion is decay'd?
We lov'd, and we lov'd, as long as we cou'd,
    Till our love was lov'd out in us both:
But our Marriage is dead, when the Pleasure is fled:
    'Twas Pleasure first made it an Oath.

If I have Pleasures for a Friend,
    And farther love in store,
What wrong has he whose joys did end,
    And who cou'd give no more?

'Tis a madness that he
Should be jealous of me,
Or that I shou'd bar him of another:
For all we can gain,
Is to give our selves pain,
When neither can hinder the other.

'Whil'st Alexis Lay Prest'

Whil'st *Alexis* lay prest
In her Arms he lov'd best,
With his hands round her neck,
And his head on her breast,
He found the fierce pleasure too hasty to stay,
And his soul in the tempest just flying away.

When *Cælia* saw this,
With a sigh, and a kiss,
She cry'd, Oh my dear, I am robb'd of my bliss;

'Tis unkind to your Love, and unfaithfully done,
To leave me behind you, and die all alone.

The Youth, though in haste,
And breathing his last,
In pity dy'd slowly, while she dy'd more fast;
Till at length she cry'd, Now, my dear, now let us go,
Now die, my *Alexis*, and I will die too.

Thus intranc'd they did lie,
Till *Alexis* did try
To recover new breath, that again he might die:
Then often they di'd; but the more they did so,
The Nymph di'd more quick, and the Shepherd more slow.

A New Song

Sylvia the fair, in the bloom of Fifteen,
Felt an innocent warmth, as she lay on the green;
She had heard of a pleasure, and something she guest
By the towzing and tumbling and touching her Breast;
She saw the men eager, but was at a loss,
What they meant by their sighing, and kissing so close;
    By their praying and whining
    And clasping and twining,
    And panting and wishing,
    And sighing and kissing,
    And sighing and kissing so close.

Ah she cry'd, ah for a languishing Maid
In a Country of Christians to die without aid!
Not a Whig, or a Tory, or Trimmer at least,
Or a Protestant Parson, or Catholick Priest,
To instruct a young Virgin, that is at a loss
What they meant by their sighing, and kissing so close!
    By their praying and whining
    And clasping and twining,
    And panting and wishing,

And sighing and kissing
And sighing and kissing so close.

Cupid in Shape of a Swayn did appear,
He saw the sad wound, and in pity drew near,
Then show'd her his Arrow, and bid her not fear,
For the pain was no more than a Maiden may bear;
When the balm was infus'd she was not at a loss,
What they meant by their sighing and kissing so close;
By their praying and whining,
And clasping and twining,
And panting and wishing,
And sighing and kissing,
And sighing and kissing so close.

Song for a Girl

Young I am, and yet unskill'd
How to make a Lover yield:
How to keep, or how to gain,
When to Love; and when to feign:

Take me, take me, some of you,
While I yet am Young and True;
E're I can my Soul disguise;
Heave my Breasts, and roul my Eyes.

Stay not till I learn the way,
How to Lye, and to Betray:
He that has me first, is blest,
For I may deceive the rest.

Cou'd I find a blooming Youth;
Full of Love, and full of Truth,
Brisk, and of a janty meen,
I shou'd long to be Fifteen.

Epilogue from *Tyrannick Love*

*Spoken by Nell Gwynne, when she was to be carried off
by the Bearers*

[*To the Bearer.*]
Hold, are you mad? you damn'd confounded Dog,
I am to rise, and speak the Epilogue.

[*To the Audience.*]
I come, kind Gentlemen, strange news to tell ye,
I am the Ghost of poor departed *Nelly*.
Sweet Ladies, be not frighted, I'le be civil,
I'm what I was, a little harmless Devil.
For after death, we Sprights, have just such Natures,
We had for all the World, when humane Creatures;
And therefore I that was an Actress here,
Play all my Tricks in Hell, a Goblin there.
Gallants, look to't, you say there are no Sprights;
But I'le come dance about your Beds at nights.
And faith you'l be in a sweet kind of taking,
When I surprise you between sleep and waking.
To tell you true, I walk because I dye
Out of my Calling in a Tragedy.
O Poet, damn'd dull Poet, who could prove
So sensless! to make *Nelly* dye for Love,
Nay, what's yet worse, to kill me in the prime
Of *Easter*-Term, in Tart and Cheese-cake time!
I'le fit the Fopp; for I'le not one word say
T'excuse his godly out of fashion Play.
A Play which if you dare but twice sit out,
You'l all be slander'd, and be thought devout.
But, farewel Gentlemen, make haste to me,
I'm sure e're long to have your company.
As for my Epitaph when I am gone,
I'le trust no Poet, but will write my own.

Here Nelly *lies, who, though she liv'd a Slater'n,*
Yet dy'd a Princess, acting in S. Cathar'n.

Prologue to *Aureng-Zebe*

Our Author by experience finds it true,
'Tis much more hard to please himself than you:
And out of no feign'd modesty, this day,
Damns his laborious Trifle of a Play:
Not that its worse than what before he writ,
But he has now another taste of Wit;
And to confess a truth, (though out of time)
Grows weary of his long-lov'd Mistris, Rhyme.
Passion's too fierce to be in Fetters bound,
And Nature flies him like Enchanted Ground.
What Verse can do, he has perform'd in this,
Which he presumes the most correct of his:
But spite of all his pride a secret shame,
Invades his breast at *Shakespear*'s sacred name:
Aw'd when he hears his Godlike *Romans* rage,
He, in a just despair, would quit the Stage.
And to an Age less polish'd, more unskill'd,
Does, with disdain the foremost Honours yield.
As with the greater Dead he dares not strive,
He wou'd not match his Verse with those who live:
Let him retire, betwixt two Ages cast,
The first of this, and hindmost of the last.
A losing Gamester, let him sneak away;
He bears no ready Money from the Play.
The Fate which governs Poets, thought it fit,
He shou'd not raise his Fortunes by his Wit.
The Clergy thrive, and the litigious Bar;
Dull Heroes fatten with the spoils of War:
All Southern Vices, Heav'n be prais'd, are here;
But Wit's a luxury you think too dear.
When you to cultivate the Plant are loath,
'Tis a shrewd sign 'twas never of your growth:
And Wit in Northern Climates will not blow,

Except, like *Orange-trees*, 'tis hous'd from Snow.
There needs no care to put a Play-house down,
'Tis the most desart place of all the Town.
We and our Neighbours, to speak proudly, are
Like Monarchs, ruin'd with expensive War.
While, like wise *English*, unconcern'd, you sit,
And see us play the Tragedy of Wit.

The Epilogue Spoken to the King at the Opening the Play-House at Oxford

As from a darkn'd Roome some Optick glass
Transmits the distant Species as they pass;
The worlds large Landschape is from far descry'd,
And men contracted on the Paper glide;
Thus crowded *Oxford* represents Mankind,
And in these Walls *Great Brittain* seems Confin'd.
Oxford is now the publick *Theater*;
And you both Audience are, and Actors here.
The gazing World on the New Scene attend,
Admire the turns, and wish a prosp'rous end.
This Place the seat of Peace, the quiet Cell
Where Arts remov'd from noisy buisness dwell,
Shou'd calm your Wills, unite the jarring parts,
And with a kind Contagion seize your hearts:
Oh! may its Genius, like soft Musick move,
And tune you all to Concord and to Love.
Our Ark that has in Tempests long been tost,
Cou'd never land on so secure a Coast.
From hence you may look back on Civil Rage,
And view the ruines of the former Age.
Here a New World its glories may unfold,
And here be sav'd the remnants of the Old.
But while your daies on publick thoughts are bent
Past ills to heal, and future to prevent;
Some vacant houres allow to your delight,
Mirth is the pleasing buisness of the Night,
The Kings Prerogative, the Peoples right.
Were all your houres to sullen cares confind,
The Body wou'd be Jaded by the Mind.
'Tis Wisdoms part betwixt extreams to Steer:
Be Gods in Senates, but be Mortals here.

from Mac Flecknoe

[Richard Flecknoe, Irish poetaster, Confers His Throne
on Thomas Shadwell]

All humane things are subject to decay,
And, when Fate summons, Monarchs must obey:
This *Fleckno* found, who, like *Augustus*, young
Was call'd to Empire, and had govern'd long:
In Prose and Verse, was own'd, without dispute
Through all the Realms of *Non-sense*, absolute.
This aged Prince now flourishing in Peace,
And blest with issue of a large increase,
Worn out with business, did at length debate
To settle the succession of the State:
And pond'ring which of all his sons was fit
To Reign, and wage immortal War with Wit;
Cry'd 'tis resolv'd; for Nature pleads that He
Should onely rule, who most resembles me:
Sh— alone my perfect image bears,
Mature in dullness from his tender years.
Sh— alone, of all my Sons, is he
Who stands confirm'd in full stupidity.
The rest to some faint meaning make pretence,
But *Sh*— never deviates into sense.
Some Beams of Wit on other souls may fall,
Strike through and make a lucid intervall;
But *Sh*—'s genuine night admits no ray,
His rising Fogs prevail upon the Day:
Besides his goodly Fabrick fills the eye,
And seems design'd for thoughtless Majesty:
Thoughtless as Monarch Oakes, that shade the plain,
And, spread in solemn state, supinely reign.

*

Now Empress *Fame* had publisht the Renown
Of *Sh*—'s Coronation through the Town.
Rows'd by report of Fame, the Nations meet,
From near *Bun-Hill*, and distant *Watling-street*.
No *Persian* Carpets spread th' Imperial way,
But scatter'd Limbs of mangled Poets lay:
From dusty shops neglected Authors come,
Martyrs of Pies, and Reliques of the Bum.
Much *Heywood*, *Shirly*, *Ogleby* there lay,
But loads of *Sh*— almost choakt the way.
Bilk't *Stationers* for Yeomen stood prepar'd,
And *H*—* was Captain of the Guard.
The hoary Prince in Majesty appear'd,
High on a Throne of his own Labours rear'd.
At his right hand our young *Ascanius* sate
Rome's other hope, and pillar of the State.
His Brows thick fogs, instead of glories, grace,
And lambent dullness plaid arround his face.
As *Hannibal* did to the Altars come,
Sworn by his *Syre* a mortal Foe to *Rome*;
So *Sh*— swore, nor should his Vow bee vain,
That he till Death true dullness would maintain;
And in his father's Right, and Realms defence,
Ne'er to have peace with Wit, nor truce with Sense.

*

The *Syre* then shook the honours of his head,
And from his brows damps of oblivion shed
Full on the filial dullness: long he stood,
Repelling from his Breast the raging God;
At length burst out in this prophetick mood:
Heavens bless my Son, from *Ireland* let him reign
To farr *Barbadoes* on the Western main;
Of his Dominion may no end be known,

* Herringman, publisher

And greater than his Father's be his Throne.
Beyond loves Kingdom let him stretch his Pen;
He paus'd, and all the people cry'd *Amen*.
Then thus, continu'd he, my Son advance
Still in new Impudence, new Ignorance ...
A Tun of Man in thy Large bulk is writ,
But sure thou'rt but a Kilderkin of wit.
Like mine thy gentle numbers feebly creep,
Thy Tragick Muse gives smiles, thy Comick sleep.
With whate'er gall thou sett'st thy self to write,
Thy inoffensive Satyrs never bite.
In thy fellonious heart, though Venom lies,
It does but touch thy *Irish* pen, and dyes.
Thy Genius calls thee not to purchase the fame
In keen Iambicks, but mild Anagram:
Leave writing Plays, and chuse for thy command
Some peacefull Province in Acrostick Land.
There thou maist wings display and Altars raise,
And torture one poor word Ten thousand ways.
Of if thou would'st thy diff'rent talents suit,
Set thy own Songs, and sing them to thy lute.
He said, but his last words were scarcely heard,
For *Bruce* and *Longvil** had a *Trap* prepar'd,
And down they sent the yet declaiming Bard.
Sinking he left his Drugget robe behind,
Born upwards by a subterranean wind.
The Mantle fell to the young Prophet's part,
With double portion of his Father's Art.

* actors

from Religio Laici
  or A Layman's Faith

Dim, as the borrow'd beams of Moon and Stars
To *lonely*, *weary*, *wandring* Travellers,
Is *Reason* to the *Soul*: And as on high,
Those rowling Fires *discover* but the Sky
Not light us *here*; So *Reason*'s glimmering Ray
Was lent, not to *assure* our *doubtfull* way,
But *guide* us upward to a *better Day*.
And as those nightly Tapers disappear
When Day's bright Lord ascends our Hemisphere;
So pale grows *Reason* at *Religions* sight;
So *dyes*, and so *dissolves* in *Supernatural Light*.
Some few, whose Lamp shone brighter, have been led
From Cause to Cause, to *Natures* secret head;
And found that *one first principle* must be:
But *what*, or *who*, that UNIVERSAL HE;
Whether some *Soul* incompassing this Ball
Unmade, *unmov'd*; yet *making*, *moving All*;
Or various *Atoms* interfering Dance
Leapt into *Form*, (the Noble work of *Chance*;)
Or this great *All* was from *Eternity*;
Not ev'n the *Stagirite* himself could see;
And *Epicurus Guess'd* as well as He:
As *blindly grop'd* they for a *future State*;
As *rashly Judg'd* of *Providence* and *Fate*:
But least of all could their Endeavours find
What most concern'd the good of Humane kind:
For *Happiness* was never to be found;
But vanish'd from 'em, like Enchanted ground.
One thought *Content* the Good to be enjoy'd:
This, every little *Accident* destroy'd:
The *wiser Madmen* did for *Vertue* toyl:
A Thorny, or at best a barren Soil:

In *Pleasure* some their glutton Souls would steep; ⎫
But found their Line too short, the Well too deep; ⎬
And leaky Vessels which no *Bliss* cou'd keep. ⎭
Thus, *anxious Thoughts* in *endless Circles* roul,
Without a *Centre* where to fix the *Soul*:
In this wilde Maze their vain Endeavours end.
How can the *less* the *Greater* comprehend?
Or *finite Reason* reach *Infinity*?
For what cou'd *Fathom GOD* were *more* than *He*.

*

  In times o'ergrown with Rust and Ignorance,
A gainfull Trade their Clergy did advance:
When want of Learning kept the *Laymen* low,
And none but *Priests* were *Authoriz'd* to *know*:
When what small Knowledge was, in them did dwell;
And he a *God* who cou'd but *Reade* or *Spell*;
Then *Mother Church* did mightily prevail:
She parcel'd out the Bible by *retail*:
But still *expounded* what She *sold* or *gave*;
To keep it in *her Power* to *Damn* and *Save*:
Scripture was *scarce*, and as the Market went,
Poor *Laymen* took *Salvation* on *Content*;
As needy men take Money, good or bad:
God's Word they had not, but the *Priests* they had.
Yet, whate'er *false Conveyances* they made,
The *Lawyer* still was *certain* to be paid.
In those dark times they learn'd their knack so well,
That by long use they grew *Infallible*:
At last, a knowing Age began t' enquire
If *they* the *Book*, or *That* did *them* inspire:
And, making narrower search they found, thô late
That what they thought the *Priest*'s, was *Their* Estate:
Taught by the *Will produc'd*, (the written Word)
How long they had been *cheated* on *Record*.
Then, every man who saw the Title fair,

Claim'd a Child's part, and put in for a Share:
Consulted Soberly his private good;
And sav'd himself as cheap as e'er he cou'd.
 'Tis true, my Friend, (and far be Flattery hence)
This good had full as bad a Consequence:
The Book thus put in every vulgar hand,
Which each presum'd he best cou'd understand,
The *Common Rule* was made the *common Prey*;
And at the mercy of the *Rabble* lay.
The tender Page with horney Fists was gaul'd;
And he was gifted most that loudest baul'd:
The *Spirit* gave the *Doctoral Degree*:
And every member of a *Company*
Was of *his Trade*, and of the *Bible free*.
Plain *Truths* enough for needfull *use* they found;
But men wou'd still be itching to *expound*:
Each was ambitious of th' obscurest place,
No measure ta'n from *Knowledge*, all from *GRACE*.
Study and *Pains* were now no more their Care;
Texts were explain'd by *Fasting*, and by *Prayer*:
This was the Fruit the *private Spirit* brought;
Occasion'd by *great Zeal*, and *little Thought*.
While Crouds unlearn'd, with rude Devotion warm,
About the Sacred Viands buz and swarm,
The *Fly-blown Text* creates a *crawling Brood*;
And turns to *Maggots* what was meant for *Food*.

To the Memory of Mr Oldham

Farewel, too little and too lately known,
Whom I began to think and call my own;
For sure our Souls were near ally'd; and thine
Cast in the same Poetick mould with mine.
One common Note on either Lyre did strike,
And Knaves and Fools we both abhorr'd alike:
To the same Goal did both our Studies drive,
The last set out the soonest did arrive.
Thus *Nisus* fell upon the slippery place,
While his young friend perform'd and won the Race.
O early ripe! to thy abundant store
What could advancing Age have added more?
It might (what Nature never gives the young)
Have taught the numbers of thy native Tongue.
But Satyr needs not those, and Wit will shine
Through the harsh cadence of a rugged line.
A noble Error, and but seldom made,
When Poets are by too much force betray'd.
Thy generous fruits, though gather'd ere their prime ⎫
Still shew'd a quickness; and maturing time ⎬
But mellows what we write to the dull sweets of Rime. ⎭
Once more, hail and farewel; farewel thou young,
But ah too short, *Marcellus* of our Tongue;
Thy Brows with Ivy, and with Laurels bound;
But Fate and gloomy Night encompass thee around.

from To the Pious Memory of the Accomplisht Young
Lady Mrs Anne Killigrew

Thou Youngest Virgin-Daughter of the Skies,
Made in the last Promotion of the Blest;
Whose Palmes, new pluckt from Paradise,
In spreading Branches more sublimely rise,
Rich with Immortal Green above the rest:
Whether, adopted to some Neighbouring Star,
Thou rol'st above us, in thy wand'ring Race,
    Or, in Procession fixt and regular,
    Mov'd with the Heavens Majestick Pace;
    Or, call'd to more Superiour Bliss,
Thou tread'st, with Seraphims, the vast Abyss:
What ever happy Region is thy place,
Cease thy Celestial Song a little space;
(Thou wilt have Time enough for Hymns Divine,
    Since Heav'ns Eternal Year is thine.)
Hear then a Mortal Muse thy Praise rehearse,
        In no ignoble Verse;
But such as thy own voice did practise here,
When thy first Fruits of Poesie were giv'n;
To make thy self a welcome Inmate there:
    While yet a young Probationer,
        And Candidate of Heav'n ...

    O Gracious God! How far have we
Prophan'd thy Heav'nly Gift of Poesy?
Made prostitute and profligate the Muse,
Debas'd to each obscene and impious use,
Whose Harmony was first ordain'd Above
For Tongues of Angels, and for Hymns of Love?
O wretched We! why were we hurry'd down
    This lubrique and adult'rate age,
    (Nay added fat Pollutions of our own)

T' increase the steaming Ordures of the Stage?
What can we say t' excuse our *Second Fall*?
Let this thy *Vestal*, Heav'n, attone for all!
Her *Arethusian* Stream remains unsoil'd,
Unmixt with Forreign Filth, and undefil'd,
Her Wit was more than Man, her Innocence a Child!

from The Hind and the Panther

[The Hind]*

A milk white *Hind*, immortal and unchang'd,
Fed on the lawns, and in the forest rang'd;
Without unspotted, innocent within,
She fear'd no danger, for she knew no sin.
Yet had she oft been chas'd with horns and hounds,
And Scythian shafts; and many winged wounds
Aim'd at Her heart; was often forc'd to fly,
And doom'd to death, though fated not to dy ...
  Panting and pensive now she rang'd alone,
And wander'd in the kingdoms, once Her own.
The common Hunt, though from their rage restrain'd
By sov'reign pow'r, her company disdain'd:
Grin'd as They pass'd, and with a glaring eye
Gave gloomy signs of secret enmity.
'Tis true, she bounded by, and trip'd so light
They had not time to take a steady sight.
For truth has such a face and such a meen
As to be lov'd needs onely to be seen.
  The bloudy *Bear* an *Independent* beast,
Unlick'd to form, in groans her hate express'd.
Among the timorous kind the *Quaking Hare*
Profess'd neutrality, but would not swear.
Next her the *Buffoon Ape*, as Atheists use,
Mimick'd all Sects, and had his own to chuse:
Still when the Lyon look'd, his knees he bent,
And pay'd at Church a Courtier's Complement.

* The Catholic Church

[Dryden's Personal Case]

What weight of antient witness can prevail
If private reason hold the publick scale?
But, gratious God, how well dost thou provide
For erring judgments an unerring Guide?
Thy throne is darkness in th' abyss of light,
A blaze of glory that forbids the sight;
O teach me to believe Thee thus conceal'd,
And search no farther than thy self reveal'd;
But her alone for my Directour take
Whom thou hast promis'd never to forsake!
My thoughtless youth was wing'd with vain desires,
My manhood, long misled by wandring fires,
Follow'd false lights; and when their glimps was gone,
My pride struck out new sparkles of her own.
Such was I, such by nature still I am,
Be thine the glory, and be mine the shame.
Good life be now my task: my doubts are done,
(What more could fright my faith, than Three in One?)
Can I believe eternal God could lye
Disguis'd in mortal mold and infancy?
That the great maker of the world could dye?
And after that, trust my imperfect sense
Which calls in question his omnipotence? ...
Rest then, my soul, from endless anguish freed;
Nor sciences thy guide, nor sense thy creed.
Faith is the best ensurer of thy bliss;
The Bank above must fail before the venture miss.

[The Persecution of the Huguenots]

From *Celtique* woods is chas'd the *wolfish* crew;
But ah! some pity e'en to brutes is due:
Their native walks, methinks, they might enjoy
Curb'd of their native malice to destroy.
Of all the tyrannies on humane kind

The worst is that which persecutes the mind.
Let us but weigh at what offence we strike,
'Tis but because we cannot think alike.
In punishing of this, we overthrow
The laws of nations and of nature too.
Beasts are the subjects of tyrannick sway,
Where still the stronger on the weaker prey.
Man onely of a softer mold is made;
Not for his fellows ruine, but their aid.
Created kind, beneficent and free,
The noble image of the Deity.
    One portion of informing fire was giv'n
To Brutes, th' inferiour family of heav'n:
The Smith divine, as with a careless beat,
Struck out the mute creation at a heat:
But, when arriv'd at last to humane race,
The god-head took a deep consid'ring space:
And, to distinguish man from all the rest,
Unlock'd the sacred treasures of his breast:
And mercy mix'd with reason did impart;
One to his head, the other to his heart:
Reason to rule, but mercy to forgive:
The first is law, the last prerogative.
And like his mind his outward form appear'd;
When issuing naked, to the wondring herd,
He charm'd their eyes, and for they lov'd, they fear'd.
Not arm'd with horns of arbitrary might,
Or claws to seize their furry spoils in fight,
Or with increase of feet t' o'ertake 'em in their flight.
Of easie shape, and pliant ev'ry way;
Confessing still the softness of his clay,
And kind as kings upon their coronation day:
With open hands, and with extended space
Of arms, to satisfie a large embrace.
Thus kneaded up with milk, the new made man
His kingdom o'er his kindred world began:

Till knowledge misapply'd, misunderstood,
And pride of Empire sour'd his balmy bloud.
Then, first rebelling, his own stamp he coins;
The murth'rer *Cain* was latent in his loins,
And bloud began its first and loudest cry
For diff'ring worship of the Deity.

[The Panther]*

The *Panther* sure the noblest, next the *Hind*,
And fairest creature of the spotted kind;
Oh, could her in-born stains be wash'd away,
She were too good to be a beast of Prey!
How can I praise, or blame, and not offend,
Or how divide the frailty from the friend!
Her faults and vertues lye so mix'd, that she
Nor wholly stands condemn'd, nor wholly free ...
Thus, like a creature of a double kind,
In her own labyrinth she lives confin'd.
To foreign lands no sound of Her is come,
Humbly content to be despis'd at home.
Such is her faith, where good cannot be had,
At least she leaves the refuse of the bad.
Nice in her choice of ill, though not of best,
And least deform'd, because reform'd the least.
In doubtfull points betwixt her diff'ring friends,
Where one for substance, one for sign contends,
Their contradicting terms she strives to join,
Sign shall be substance, substance shall be sign.

[The Swallows]†

The *Swallow*, privileg'd above the rest
Of all the birds, as man's familiar Guest,

* The Anglican Church
† The uncertainties of English Catholics under James II

32

Pursues the Sun in summer brisk and bold,
But wisely shuns the persecuting cold:
Is well to chancels and to chimneys known,
Though 'tis not thought she feeds on smoak alone.
From hence she has been held of heav'nly line,
Endu'd with particles of soul divine.
This merry Chorister had long possess'd
Her summer seat, and feather'd well her nest:
Till frowning skys began to change their chear
And time turn'd up the wrong side of the year;
The shedding trees began the ground to strow
With yellow leaves, and bitter blasts to blow.
Sad auguries of winter thence she drew,
Which by instinct, or Prophecy, she knew:
When prudence warn'd her to remove betimes
And seek a better heav'n, and warmer clymes.

   Her sons were summon'd on a steeples height,
And, call'd in common council, vote a flight;
The day was nam'd, the next that shou'd be fair,
All to the gen'ral rendezvous repair,
They try their flutt'ring wings and trust themselves in air.
But whether upward to the moon they go,
Or dream the winter out in caves below,
Or hawk at flies elsewhere, concerns us not to know.

   Southwards, you may be sure, they bent their flight,
And harbour'd in a hollow rock at night:
Next morn they rose and set up ev'ry sail,
The wind was fair, but blew a *mackrel* gale:
The sickly young sat shivring on the shoar,
Abhorr'd salt-water never seen before,
And pray'd their tender mothers to delay
The passage, and expect a fairer day.

A Song for St Cecilia's Day, 1687

I

From Harmony, from heav'nly Harmony
    This universal Frame began.
  When Nature underneath a heap
    Of jarring Atomes lay,
  And cou'd not heave her Head,
The tuneful Voice was heard from high,
    Arise ye more than dead.
Then cold, and hot, and moist, and dry,
In order to their stations leap,
    And MUSICK's pow'r obey.
From Harmony, from heav'nly Harmony
    This universal Frame began:
    From Harmony to Harmony
Through all the compass of the Notes it ran,
The Diapason closing full in Man.

II

What Passion cannot MUSICK raise and quell!
    When *Jubal* struck the corded Shell,
  His list'ning Brethren stood around
  And wond'ring, on their Faces fell
  To worship that Celestial Sound.
Less than a God they thought there cou'd not dwell
    Within the hollow of that Shell
    That spoke so sweetly and so well.
What Passion cannot MUSICK raise and quell!

III

  The TRUMPETS loud Clangor
    Excites us to Arms

With shrill Notes of Anger
  And mortal Alarms.
The double double double beat
  Of the thundring DRUM
Cryes, heark the Foes come;
Charge, Charge, 'tis too late to retreat.

IV

The soft complaining FLUTE
In dying Notes discovers
The Woes of hopeless Lovers,
Whose Dirge is whisper'd by the warbling LUTE.

V

Sharp VIOLINS proclaim
Their jealous Pangs, and Desperation,
Fury, frantick Indignation,
Depth of Pains, and height of Passion,
  For the fair, disdainful Dame.

VI

But oh! what Art can teach
What human Voice can reach
The sacred ORGANS praise?
Notes inspiring holy Love,
Notes that wing their heav'nly ways
  To mend the Choires above.

VII

Orpheus cou'd lead the savage race;
And Trees unrooted left their place;
  Sequacious of the Lyre:
But bright *CECILIA* rais'd the wonder high'r;
When to her ORGAN, vocal Breath was giv'n

An Angel heard, and straight appear'd
    Mistaking Earth for Heaven.

Grand CHORUS

As from the pow'r of sacred Lays
    The Spheres began to move,
And sung the great Creator's praise
    To all the bless'd above;
So when the last and dreadful hour
This crumbling Pageant shall devour,
The TRUMPET shall be heard on high,
The Dead shall live, the Living die,
And MUSICK shall untune the Sky.

Lines on Milton

Three *Poets*, in three distant *Ages* born,
Greece, *Italy*, and *England* did adorn.
The *First* in loftiness of thought Surpass'd;
The *Next* in Majesty; in both the *Last*.
The force of *Nature* cou'd no farther goe:
To make a *Third* she joynd the former two.

from Eleonora: A Panegyrical Poem to the Memory of the Late Countess of Abingdon

[The Babe]

The Babe had all that Infant care beguiles,
And early knew his Mother in her smiles:
But when dilated Organs let in day
To the young Soul, and gave it room to play,
At his first aptness, the Maternal Love
Those Rudiments of Reason did improve:
The tender Age was pliant to command;
Like Wax it yielded to the forming hand:
True to th' Artificer, the labour'd Mind
With ease was pious, generous, just and kind;
Soft for Impression from the first, prepar'd,
Till Vertue, with long exercise, grew hard;
With ev'ry Act confirm'd; and made, at last
So durable, as not to be effac'd,
It turn'd to Habit; and, from Vices free,
Goodness resolv'd into Necessity.

Reflections on the Shortness of Her Life

Tho all these rare Endowments of the Mind
Were in a narrow space of life confin'd;
The Figure was with full Perfection crown'd;
Though not so large an Orb, as truly round.
    As when in glory, through the publick place,
The Spoils of conquer'd Nations were to pass,
And but one Day for Triumph was allow'd,
The Consul was constrain'd his Pomp to crowd;
And so the swift Procession hurry'd on,
That all, though not distinctly, might be shown;
So, in the straiten'd bounds of life confin'd,
She gave but glimpses of her glorious Mind:

And multitudes of Vertues pass'd along;
Each pressing foremost in the mighty throng;
Ambitious to be seen, and then make room,
For greater Multitudes that were to come.

Yet unemploy'd no Minute slipt away;
Moments were precious in so short a stay.
The haste of Heav'n to have her was so great,
That some were single Acts, though each compleat;
But ev'ry Act stood ready to repeat.

The Manner of Her Death

A short sweet Odour, of a vast expence.
She vanish'd, we can scarcely say she dy'd;
For but a Now, did Heav'n and Earth divide:
She pass'd serenely with a single breath,
This Moment perfect health, the next was death.
One sigh, did her eternal Bliss assure;
So little Penance needs, when Souls are almost pure.
As gentle Dreams our waking Thoughts pursue;
Or, one Dream pass'd, we slide into a new;
(So close they follow, such wild Order keep,
We think our selves awake, and are asleep:)
So softly death succeeded life, in her;
She did but dream of Heav'n, and she was there.

from To My Dear Friend Mr Congreve,
on His Comedy, call'd *The Double-Dealer*

Well then; the promis'd hour is come at last;
The present Age of Wit obscures the past:
Strong were our Syres; and as they Fought they Writ,
Conqu'ring with force of Arms, and dint of Wit;
Theirs was the Gyant Race, before the Flood;
And thus, when *Charles* Return'd, our Empire stood.
Like *Janus* he the stubborn Soil manur'd,
With Rules of Husbandry the rankness cur'd:
Tam'd us to manners, when the Stage was rude;
And boistrous *English* Wit, with Art indu'd.
Our Age was cultivated thus at length;
But what we gain'd in skill we lost in strength.
Our Builders were, with want of Genius, curst;
The second Temple was not like the first:
Till You, the best *Vitruvius*, come at length;
Our Beauties equal; but excel our strength.
Firm *Dorique* Pillars found Your solid Base:
The Fair *Corinthian* Crowns the higher Space;
Thus all below is Strength, and all above is Grace ...

    Oh that your Brows my Lawrel had sustain'd,
Well had I been Depos'd, if You had reign'd!
The Father had descended for the Son;
For only You are lineal to the Throne.
Thus when the State one *Edward* did depose;
A Greater *Edward* in his room arose.
But now, not I, but Poetry is curs'd;
For *Tom* the Second reigns like *Tom* the first ...
Already I am worn with Cares and Age;
And just abandoning th' Ungrateful Stage:
Unprofitably kept at Heav'ns expence,
I live a Rent-charge on his Providence:
But You, whom ev'ry Muse and Grace adorn,

Whom I foresee to better Fortune born,
Be kind to my Remains; and oh defend,
Against Your Judgment, Your departed Friend!
Let not the Insulting Foe my Fame pursue;
But shade those Lawrels which descend to You:
And take for Tribute what these Lines express:
You merit more; nor cou'd my Love do less.

Alexander's Feast; or The Power of Musique
An Ode, in Honour of St Cecilia's Day

I

'Twas at the Royal Feast, for *Persia* won,
      By *Philip*'s Warlike Son:
  Aloft in awful State
  The God-like Heroe sate
    On his Imperial Throne:
  His valiant Peers were plac'd around;
Their Brows with Roses and with Myrtles bound.
  (So shou'd Desert in Arms be Crown'd:)
The Lovely *Thais* by his side,
Sate like a blooming *Eastern* Bride
In Flow'r of Youth and Beauty's Pride.
    Happy, happy, happy Pair!
    None but the Brave
    None but the Brave
    None but the Brave deserves the Fair.

CHORUS

    Happy, happy, happy Pair!
    None but the Brave
    None but the Brave
    None but the Brave deserves the Fair.

II

Timotheus plac'd on high
  Amid the tuneful Quire,
  With flying Fingers touch'd the Lyre:
The trembling Notes ascend the sky,
          And Heav'nly Joys inspire.
The Song began from *Jove*;

Who left his blissful Seats above,
(Such is the Pow'r of mighty Love.)
A Dragon's fiery Form bely'd the God:
Sublime on Radiant Spires He rode,
      When He to fair *Olympia* press'd:
      And while He sought her snowy Breast:
Then, round her slender Waste he curl'd,
And stamp'd an Image of himself, a Sov'raign of the World.
The list'ning Crowd admire the lofty Sound,
A present Deity, they shout around:
A present Deity the vaulted Roofs rebound.
            With ravish'd Ears
            The Monarch hears,
            Assumes the God,
            Affects to nod,
      And seems to shake the Spheres.

CHORUS

      With ravish'd Ears
      The Monarch hears,
      Assumes the God,
      Affects to nod,
And seems to shake the Spheres.

III

The Praise of *Bacchus* then, the sweet Musician sung;
   Of *Bacchus* ever Fair, and ever Young:
      The jolly God in Triumph comes;
      Sound the Trumpets; beat the Drums:
         Flush'd with a purple Grace
         He shews his honest Face,
Now give the Hautboys breath; He comes, He comes.
      Bacchus ever Fair and Young,
         Drinking Joys did first ordain:
      Bacchus Blessings are a Treasure;

Drinking is the Soldiers Pleasure;
    Rich the Treasure,
    Sweet the Pleasure;
Sweet is Pleasure after Pain.

CHORUS

Bacchus *Blessings are a Treasure;*
Drinking is the Soldier's Pleasure;
    Rich the Treasure,
    Sweet the Pleasure;
Sweet is Pleasure after Pain.

IV

Sooth'd with the Sound the King grew vain;
    Fought all his Battails o'er again;
And thrice He routed all his Foes; and thrice He slew the slain.
    The Master saw the Madness rise;
    His glowing Cheeks, his ardent Eyes;
    And while He Heav'n and Earth defy'd,
    Chang'd his hand, and check'd his Pride.
      He chose a Mournful Muse
      Soft Pity to infuse:
    He sung *Darius* Great and Good,
      By too severe a Fate,
    Fallen, fallen, fallen, fallen,
      Fallen from his high Estate
        And weltring in his Blood:
Deserted at his utmost Need,
By those his former Bounty fed:
On the bare Earth expos'd He lyes,
With not a Friend to close his Eyes.

With down-cast Looks the joyless Victor sate,
    Revolveing in his alter'd Soul
      The various Turns of Chance below;

And, now and then, a Sigh he stole;
   And Tears began to flow.

CHORUS

Revolveing in his alter'd Soul
   The various Turns of Chance below;
And, now and then, a Sigh he stole;
   And Tears began to flow.

V

The Mighty Master smil'd to see
That Love was in the next Degree:
'Twas but a Kindred-Sound to move;
For Pity melts the Mind to Love.
   Softly sweet, in *Lydian* Measures,
   Soon He sooth'd his Soul to Pleasures.
   War, he sung, is Toil and Trouble;
   Honour but an empty Bubble.
     Never ending, still beginning,
   Fighting still, and still destroying,
     If the World be worth thy Winning,
   Think, O think, it worth Enjoying.
     Lovely *Thais* sits beside thee,
     Take the Good the Gods provide thee.

The Many rend the Skies, with loud Applause;
So Love was Crown'd, but Musique won the Cause.
   The Prince, unable to conceal his Pain,
       Gaz'd on the Fair
       Who caus'd his Care,
   And sigh'd and look'd, sigh'd and look'd,
   Sigh'd and look'd, and sigh'd again:
At length, with Love and Wine at once oppress'd,
The vanquish'd Victor sunk upon her Breast.

The Prince, unable to conceal his Pain,
  Gaz'd on the Fair
  Who caus'd his Care,
 And sigh'd and look'd, sigh'd and look'd,
Sigh'd and look'd, and sigh'd again:
At length, with Love and Wine at once oppress'd,
The vanquish'd Victor sunk upon her Breast.

VI

Now strike the Golden Lyre again:
A lowder yet, and yet a lowder Strain.
Break his Bands of Sleep asunder,
And rouze him, like a rattling Peal of Thunder.
  Hark, hark, the horrid Sound
   Has rais'd up his Head,
   As awak'd from the Dead,
  And amaz'd, he stares around.
Revenge, Revenge, *Timotheus* cries,
 See the Furies arise!
 See the Snakes that they rear,
 How they hiss in their Hair,
And the Sparkles that flash from their Eyes!
 Behold a ghastly Band,
 Each a Torch in his Hand!
Those are *Grecian* Ghosts, that in Battail were slayn,
     And unbury'd remain
     Inglorious on the Plain.
  Give the Vengeance due
  To the Valiant Crew.
Behold how they toss their Torches on high,
 How they point to the *Persian* Abodes,
And glitt'ring Temples of their Hostile Gods!
The Princes applaud, with a furious Joy;
And the King seyz'd a Flambeau, with Zeal to destroy;

> *Thais* led the Way,
> To light him to his Prey,
And, like another *Hellen*, fir'd another *Troy*.

CHORUS

And the King seyz'd a Flambeau, with Zeal to destroy;
> Thais *led the Way,*
> *To light him to his Prey,*
And, like another Hellen, *fir'd another* Troy.

VII

Thus, long ago
'Ere heaving Bellows learn'd to blow,
While Organs yet were mute;
Timotheus, to his breathing Flute,
And sounding Lyre,
Cou'd swell the Soul to rage, or kindle soft Desire.
At last Divine *Cecilia* came,
Inventress of the Vocal Frame;
The sweet Enthusiast, from her Sacred Store,
Enlarg'd the former narrow Bounds,
And added Length to solemn Sounds,
With Nature's Mother-Wit, and Arts unknown before.
Let old *Timotheus* yield the Prize,
Or both divide the Crown;
He rais'd a Mortal to the Skies;
She drew an Angel down.

Grand CHORUS

At last Divine Cecilia *came,*
Inventress of the Vocal Frame;
The sweet Enthusiast, from her Sacred Store,
Enlarg'd the former narrow Bounds,
And added Length to solemn Sounds,

47

With Nature's Mother-Wit, and Arts unknown before.
   Let old Timotheus yield the Prize,
     Or both divide the Crown;
   He rais'd a Mortal to the Skies;
     She drew an Angel down.

The Secular Masque

> *Enter* Janus.

Janus.   *Chronos, Chronos,* mend thy Pace,
An hundred times the rowling Sun
Around the Radiant Belt has run
In his revolving Race.
Behold, behold, the Goal in sight,
Spread thy Fans, and wing thy flight.

> *Enter* Chronos, *with a Scythe in his hand, and
> a great Globe on his Back, which he sets down at
> his entrance.*

Chronos.   Weary, weary of my weight,
Let me, let me drop my Freight,
　　And leave the World behind.
I could not bear
Another Year
The Load of Human-Kind.

> *Enter* Momus *Laughing.*

Momus.   Ha! ha! ha! Ha! ha! ha! well hast thou done,
　　To lay down thy Pack,
　　And lighten thy Back,
The World was a Fool, e'er since it begun,
And since neither *Janus,* nor *Chronos,* nor I,
　　Can hinder the Crimes,
　　Or mend the Bad Times,
'Tis better to Laugh than to Cry.
Cho. of all 3. *'Tis better to Laugh than to Cry.*
Janus.   Since *Momus* comes to laugh below,
　　Old Time begin the Show,
That he may see, in every Scene,
What Changes in this Age have been,

Chronos.	Then Goddess of the Silver Bow begin.
	Horns, or Hunting-Musique within.
	Enter Diana.
Diana.	With Horns and with Hounds I waken the Day,
	And hye to my Woodland walks away;
	I tuck up my Robe, and am buskin'd soon,
	And tye to my Forehead a wexing Moon.
	I course the fleet Stagg, unkennel the Fox,
	And chase the wild Goats or'e summets of Rocks,
	With shouting and hooting we pierce thro' the Sky;
	And Eccho turns Hunter, and doubles the Cry.
Cho. of all.	*With shouting and hooting, we pierce through the*
	Skie,
	And Eccho turns Hunter, and doubles the Cry.
Janus.	Then our Age was in it's Prime,
Chronos.	Free from Rage.
Diana.	—————And free from Crime.
Momus.	A very Merry, Dancing, Drinking,
	Laughing, Quaffing, and unthinking Time.
Cho. of all.	*Then our Age was in it's Prime,*
	Free from Rage, and free from Crime,
	A very Merry, Dancing, Drinking,
	Laughing, Quaffing, and unthinking Time.
	Dance of Diana's *Attendants.*
	Enter Mars.
Mars.	Inspire the Vocal Brass, Inspire;
	The World is past its Infant Age:
	Arms and Honour,
	Arms and Honour,
	Set the Martial Mind on Fire,
	And kindle Manly Rage.
	Mars has lookt the Sky to Red;
	And Peace, the Lazy Good, is fled.

Plenty, Peace, and Pleasure fly;
   The Sprightly Green
In *Woodland*-Walks, no more is seen;
The Sprightly Green, has drunk the *Tyrian* Dye.

Cho. of all.	*Plenty, Peace,* &c.
Mars.	Sound the Trumpet, Beat the Drum,

Through all the World around;
Sound a Reveille, Sound, Sound,
   The Warrior God is come.

Cho. of all.	*Sound the Trumpet,* &c.
Momus.	Thy Sword within the Scabbard keep,

   And let Mankind agree;
Better the World were fast asleep,
   Than kept awake by Thee.
The Fools are only thinner,
   With all our Cost and Care;
But neither side a winner,
   For Things are as they were.

Cho. of all.	*The Fools are only,* &c.

Enter Venus.

Venus.	Calms appear, when Storms are past;

Love will have his Hour at last:
Nature is my kindly Care;
Mars destroys, and I repair;
Take me, take me, while you may,
Venus comes not ev'ry Day.

Cho. of all.	*Take her, take her,* &c.
Chronos.	The World was then so light,

I scarcely felt the Weight;
Joy rul'd the Day, and Love the Night.
But since the Queen of Pleasure left the Ground,
   I faint, I lag,
   And feebly drag
The pond'rous Orb around.

Momus.	All, all, of a piece throughout;

Pointing to *Diana*. }	Thy Chase had a Beast in View;
to *Mars*.	Thy Wars brought nothing about;
to *Venus*.	Thy Lovers were all untrue.
Janus.	'Tis well an Old Age is out,
Chro[nos].	And time to begin a New.
Cho. of all.	*All, all, of a piece throughout;*
	Thy Chase had a Beast in View;
	Thy Wars brought nothing about;
	Thy Lovers were all untrue.
	'Tis well an Old Age is out,
	And time to begin a New.

Dance of Huntsmen, Nymphs, Warriours and Lovers.

TRANSLATIONS

from The Iliad, Book I

[The Invocation]

The wrath of *Peleus* Son, O Muse, resound;
Whose dire Effects the *Grecian* Army found:
And many a Heroe, King, and hardy Knight,
Were sent in early Youth, to Shades of Night:
Their Limbs a Prey to Dogs and Vulturs made;
So was the Sov'reign Will of *Jove* obey'd:
From that ill-omen'd Hour when Strife begun,
Betwixt *Atrides* Great, and *Thetis* God-like Son.

[Achilles, Threatened by Agamemnon]

At this th' Impatient Hero sowrly smil'd:
His Heart, impetuous in his Bosom boil'd,
And justled by two Tides of equal sway,
Stood, for a while, suspended in his way.
Betwixt his Reason, and his Rage untam'd;
One whisper'd soft, and one aloud reclaim'd:
That only counsell'd to the safer side;
This to the Sword, his ready Hand apply'd.
Unpunish'd to support th' Affront was hard:
Nor easy was th' Attempt to force the Guard.
But soon the thirst of Vengeance fir'd his Blood:
Half shone his Faulchion, and half sheath'd it stood.
In that nice moment, *Pallas*, from above,
Commission'd by th' Imperial Wife of *Jove*,
Descended swift: (the white arm'd Queen was loath
The Fight shou'd follow; for she favour'd both:)
Just as in Act he stood, in Clouds inshrin'd,
Her Hand she fasten'd on his Hair behind;
Then backward by his yellow Curls she drew:

To him, and him alone confess'd in view.
Tam'd by superiour Force he turn'd his Eyes
Aghast at first, and stupid with Surprize.

[Achilles' Wrath]

At her departure his Disdain return'd:
The Fire she fan'd, with greater Fury burn'd;
Rumbling within till thus it found a vent:
Dastard, and Drunkard, Mean and Insolent:
Tongue-valiant Hero, Vaunter of thy Might,
In Threats the foremost, but the lag in Fight;
When did'st thou thrust amid the mingled Preace,
Content to bid the War aloof in Peace?
Arms are the Trade of each *Plebeyan* Soul;
'Tis Death to fight; but Kingly to controul.
Lord-like at ease, with arbitrary Pow'r,
To peel the Chiefs, the People to devour.
These, Traitor, are thy Tallents; safer far
Than to contend in Fields, and Toils of War.
Nor coud'st thou thus have dar'd the common Hate,
Were not their Souls as abject as their State.
But, by this Scepter, solemnly I swear,
(Which never more green Leaf or growing Branch shall bear:
Torn from the Tree, and giv'n by *Jove* to those
Who Laws dispence and mighty Wrongs oppose)
That when the *Grecians* want my wonted Aid,
No Gift shall bribe it, and no Pray'r persuade.

[The Sacrifice to Apollo]

Now when the solemn Rites of Pray'r were past,
Their salted Cakes on crackling Flames they cast.
Then, turning back, the Sacrifice they sped:
The fatted Oxen slew, and flea'd the Dead.
Chop'd off their nervous Thighs, and next prepar'd
T' involve the lean in Cauls, and mend with Lard.

Sweet-breads and Collops, were with Skewers prick'd
About the Sides; inbibing what they deck'd.
The Priest with holy Hands was seen to tine
The cloven Wood, and pour the ruddy Wine.
The Youth approach'd the Fire and as it burn'd
On five sharp Broachers rank'd, the Roast they turn'd:
These Morsels stay'd their Stomachs; then the rest
They cut in Legs and Fillets for the Feast;
Which drawn and serv'd, their Hunger they appease
With sav'ry Meat, and set their Minds at ease.

Now when the rage of Eating was repell'd,
The Boys with generous Wine the Goblets fill'd.
The first Libations to the Gods they pour:
And then with Songs indulge the Genial Hour.
Holy Debauch! Till Day to Night they bring,
With Hymns and *Pæans* to the Bowyer King.
At Sun-set to their Ship they make return,
And snore secure on Decks, till rosy Morn.

[Thetis Asks Jove to Revenge Her Son Achilles]

Now, when twelve Days compleat had run their Race,
The Gods bethought them of the Cares belonging to their place.
Jove at their Head ascending from the Sea,
A shoal of puny Pow'rs attend his way.
Then *Thetis* not unmindful of her Son
Emerging from the Deep, to beg her Boon,
Pursu'd their Track; and waken'd from his rest,
Before the Soveraign stood a Morning Guest.
Him in the Circle but apart, she found:
The rest at awful distance stood around.
She bow'd, and e'er she durst her Sute begin,
One Hand embrac'd his Knees, one prop'd his Chin.
Then thus. If I, Celestial Sire, in aught
Have serv'd thy Will, or gratify'd thy Thought,
One glimpse of Glory to my Issue give;

Grac'd for the little time he has to live.
Dishonour'd by the King of Men he stands:
His rightful Prize is ravish'd from his Hands.
But thou, O Father, in my Son's Defence,
Assume thy Pow'r, assert thy Providence.
Let *Troy* prevail, till *Greece* th' Affront has paid,
With doubled Honours; and redeem'd his Aid.

She ceas'd, but the consid'ring God was mute:
'Till she resolv'd to win, renew'd her Sute:
Nor loos'd her Hold, but forc'd him to reply,
Or grant me my Petition, or deny:
Jove cannot fear: Then tell me to my Face
That I, of all the Gods am least in grace.
This I can bear: The Cloud-Compeller mourn'd,
And sighing, first, this Answer he return'd.

Know'st thou what Clamors will disturb my Reign,
What my stun'd Ears from *Juno* must sustain?
In Council she gives Licence to her Tongue,
Loquacious, Brawling, ever in the wrong.
And now she will my partial Pow'r upbraid,
If alienate from *Greece*, I give the *Trojans* Aid.
But thou depart, and shun her jealous Sight,
The Care be mine, to do *Pelides* right.
Go then, and on the Faith of *Jove* rely;
When nodding to thy Sute, he bows the Sky.
This ratifies th' irrevocable Doom:
The Sign ordain'd, that what I will shall come:
The Stamp of Heav'n, and Seal of Fate: He said,
And shook the sacred Honours of his Head.
With Terror trembled Heav'ns subsiding Hill:
And from his shaken Curls Ambrosial Dews distil.
The Goddess goes exulting from his Sight,
And seeks the Seas profound; and leaves the Realms of Light.

He moves into his Hall: The Pow'rs resort,
Each from his House to fill the Soveraign's Court.
Nor waiting Summons, nor expecting stood;

But met with Reverence, and receiv'd the God.
He mounts the Throne; and *Juno* took her place:
But sullen Discontent sate lowring on her Face.
With jealous Eyes, at distance she had seen,
Whisp'ring with *Jove* the Silver-footed Queen;
Then, impotent of Tongue (her Silence broke)
Thus turbulent in rattling Tone she spoke.

    Author of Ills, and close Contriver *Jove*,
Which of thy Dames, what Prostitute of Love,
Has held thy Ear so long and begg'd so hard
For some old Service done, some new Reward?
Apart you talk'd, for that's your special care
The Consort never must the Council share.
One gracious Word is for a Wife too much:
Such is a Marriage-Vow, and *Jove*'s own Faith is such.

    Then thus the Sire of Gods, and Men below,
What I have hidden, hope not thou to know.
Ev'n Goddesses are Women: And no Wife
Has Pow'r to regulate her Husband's Life:
Counsel she may; and I will give thy Ear
The Knowledge first, of what is fit to hear.
What I transact with others, or alone,
Beware to learn; nor press too near the Throne.

    To whom the Goddess with the charming Eyes,
What hast thou said, O Tyrant of the Skies,
When did I search the Secrets of thy Reign,
Though priviledg'd to know, but priviledg'd in vain?
But well thou dost, to hide from common Sight
Thy close Intrigues, too bad to bear the Light.
Nor doubt I, but the Silver-footed Dame,
Tripping from Sea, on such an Errand came,
To grace her Issue, at the *Grecians* Cost,
And for one peevish Man destroy an Host.

    To whom the Thund'rer made this stern Reply;
My Household Curse, my lawful Plague, the Spy
Of *Jove*'s Designs, his other squinting Eye;

Why this vain prying, and for what avail?
Jove will be Master still and *Juno* fail.
Shou'd thy suspicious Thoughts divine aright,
Thou but becom'st more odious to my Sight,
For this Attempt: uneasy Life to me
Still watch'd, and importun'd, but worse for thee.
Curb that impetuous Tongue, before too late
The Gods behold, and tremble at thy Fate.
Pitying, but daring not in thy Defence,
To lift a Hand against Omnipotence.

   This heard, the Imperious Queen sate mute with Fear;
Nor further durst incense the gloomy Thunderer.
Silence was in the Court at this Rebuke:
Nor cou'd the Gods abash'd, sustain their Sov'reigns Look.

   The Limping Smith, observ'd the sadden'd Feast;
And hopping here and there (himself a Jest).
Put in his Word, that neither might offend;
To *Jove* obsequious, yet his Mother's Friend.
What end in Heav'n will be of civil War,
If Gods of Pleasure will for Mortals jar?
Such Discord but disturbs our Jovial Feast;
One Grain of Bad, embitters all the best.
Mother, tho' wise your self, my Counsel weigh;
'Tis much unsafe my Sire to disobey.
Not only you provoke him to your Cost,
But Mirth is marr'd, and the good Chear is lost.
Tempt not his heavy Hand; for he has Pow'r
To throw you Headlong, from his Heav'nly Tow'r.
But one submissive Word, which you let fall,
Will make him in good Humour with us All.

   He said no more but crown'd a Bowl, unbid:
The laughing Nectar overlook'd the Lid:
Then put it to her Hand; and thus pursu'd,
This cursed Quarrel be no more renew'd.
Be, as becomes a Wife, obedient still;
Though griev'd, yet subject to her Husband's Will.

I wou'd not see you beaten; yet affraid
Of *Jove*'s superiour Force, I dare not aid.
Too well I know him, since that hapless Hour
When I, and all the Gods employ'd our Pow'r
To break your Bonds: Me by the Heel he drew;
And o'er Heav'n's Battlements with Fury threw.
All Day I fell; My Flight at Morn begun,
And ended not but with the setting Sun.
Pitch'd on my Head, at length the *Lemnian*-ground
Receiv'd my batter'd Skull, the *Sinthians* heal'd my Wound.
   At *Vulcan*'s homely Mirth his Mother smil'd,
And smiling took the Cup the Clown had fill'd.
The Reconciler Bowl, went round the Board,
Which empty'd, the rude Skinker still restor'd.
Loud Fits of Laughter seiz'd the Guests, to see
The limping God so deft at his new Ministry.
The Feast continu'd till declining Light:
They drank, they laugh'd, they lov'd, and then 'twas Night.
Nor wanted tuneful Harp, nor vocal Quire;
The Muses sung; *Apollo* touch'd the Lyre.
Drunken at last, and drowsy they depart,
Each to his House; Adorn'd with labour'd Art
Of the lame Architect: The thund'ring God
Ev'n he withdrew to rest, and had his Load.
His swimming Head to needful Sleep apply'd;
And *Juno* lay unheeded by his Side.

The Last Parting of Hector and Andromache
From the Sixth Book of Homer's Iliads

Thus having said, brave *Hector* went to see
His Virtuous Wife, the fair *Andromache*.
He found her not at home; for she was gone
(Attended by her Maid and Infant Son,)
To climb the steepy Tow'r of *Ilion*:
From whence with heavy Heart she might survey
The bloody business of the dreadful Day.
Her mournful Eyes she cast around the Plain,
And sought the Lord of her Desires in vain.

But he, who thought his peopled Palace bare,
When she, his only Comfort, was not there;
Stood in the Gate, and ask'd of ev'ry one,
Which way she took, and whither she was gone:
If to the Court, or with his Mother's Train,
In long Procession to *Minerva*'s Fane?
The Servants answer'd, neither to the Court
Where *Priam*'s Sons and Daughters did resort,
Nor to the Temple was she gone, to move
With Prayers the blew-ey'd Progeny of *Jove*;
But, more solicitous for him alone,
Than all their safety, to the Tow'r was gone,
There to survey the Labours of the Field;
Where the *Greeks* conquer, and the *Trojans* yield.
Swiftly she pass'd, with Fear and Fury wild,
The Nurse went lagging after with the Child.

This heard, the Noble *Hector* made no stay;
Th' admiring Throng divide, to give him way:
He pass'd through every Street, by which he came,
And at the Gate he met the mournful Dame.

His Wife beheld him, and with eager pace,
Flew to his *Arms*, to meet a dear Embrace:
His Wife, who brought in Dow'r *Cilicia*'s Crown;

And, in her self, a greater Dow'r alone:
Aëtion's Heyr, who on the Woody Plain
Of *Hippoplacus* did in *Thebe* reign.
Breathless she flew, with Joy and Passion wild,
The Nurse came lagging after with her Child.

The *Royal Babe* upon her *Breast* was laid;
Who, like the Morning Star, his beams display'd.
Scamandrius was his Name which *Hector* gave,
From that fair Flood which *Ilion*'s Wall did lave:
But him *Astyanax* the *Trojans* call,
From his great Father who defends the Wall.

Hector beheld him with a silent Smile,
His tender Wife stood weeping by, the while:
Prest in her own, his Warlike hand she took,
Then sigh'd, and thus Prophetically spoke.

Thy dauntless Heart (which I foresee too late,)
Too daring Man, will urge thee to thy Fate:
Nor dost thou pity, with a Parent's mind,
This helpless Orphan whom thou leav'st behind;
Nor me, th' unhappy Partner of thy *Bed*;
Who must in Triumph by the *Greeks* be led:
They seek thy Life; and in unequal Fight,
With many will oppress thy single Might:
Better it were for miserable me
To die before the Fate which I foresee.
For ah what comfort can the World bequeath
To *Hector*'s Widow, after *Hector*'s death!

Eternal Sorrow and perpetual Tears
Began my Youth, and will conclude my Years:
I have no Parents, Friends, nor Brothers left;
By stern *Achilles* all of Life bereft.
Then when the Walls of *Thebes* he o'rethrew,
His fatal Hand my Royal Father slew;
He slew *Aëtion*, but despoil'd him not;
Nor in his hate the Funeral Rites forgot;
Arm'd as he was he sent him whole below;

And reverenc'd thus the Manes of his Foe:
A Tomb he rais'd; the Mountain Nymphs around,
Enclos'd with planted Elms the Holy Ground.
    My sev'n brave *Brothers* in one fatal Day
To Death's dark Mansions took the mournful way:
Slain by the same *Achilles*, while they keep
The bellowing Oxen and the bleating Sheep.
My Mother, who the Royal Scepter sway'd,
Was Captive to the cruel Victor made:
And hither led: but hence redeem'd with Gold,
Her Native Country did again behold.
And but beheld: for soon *Diana*'s Dart
In an unhappy Chace transfix'd her Heart.
    But thou, my *Hector*, art thy self alone,
My Parents, Brothers, and my Lord in one:
O kill not all my Kindred o're again,
Nor tempt the Dangers of the dusty Plain;
But in this Tow'r, for our Defence, remain.
Thy Wife and Son are in thy Ruin lost:
This is a Husband's and a Father's Post.
The *Scæan* Gate commands the Plains below;
Here marshal all thy Souldiers as they go;
And hence, with other Hands, repel the Foe.
By yon wild Fig-tree lies their chief ascent,
And thither all their Pow'rs are daily bent:
The two *Ajaces* have I often seen,
And the wrong'd Husband of the *Spartan* Queen:
With him his greater *Brother*; and with these
Fierce *Diomede* and bold *Meriones*:
Uncertain if by *Augury*, or chance,
But by this easie rise they all advance;
Guard well that Pass, secure of all beside.
To whom the Noble *Hector* thus reply'd.
    That and the rest are in my daily care;
But shou'd I shun the Dangers of the War,
With scorn the *Trojans* wou'd reward my pains,

And their proud Ladies with their sweeping Trains.
The *Grecian* Swords and Lances I can bear:
But loss of Honour is my only Fear.
Shall *Hector*, born to War, his *Birth-right* yield,
Belie his Courage and forsake the Field?
Early in rugged *Arms* I took delight;
And still have been the foremost in the Fight:
With dangers dearly have I bought Renown,
And am the Champion of my Father's Crown.

   And yet my mind forebodes, with sure presage,
That *Troy* shall perish by the *Grecian* Rage.
The fatal Day draws on, when I must fall;
And Universal Ruine cover all.
Not *Troy* it self, tho' built by Hands Divine,
Nor *Priam*, nor his People, nor his Line,
My Mother, nor my *Brothers* of Renown,
Whose Valour yet defends th' unhappy Town,
Not these, nor all their Fates which I foresee,
Are half of that concern I have for thee.
I see, I see thee in that fatal Hour,
Subjected to the Victor's cruel Pow'r:
Led hence a Slave to some insulting Sword:
Forlorn and trembling at a Foreign Lord.
A spectacle in *Argos*, at the Loom,
Gracing with *Trojan* Fights, a *Grecian* Room;
Or from deep Wells, the living Stream to take,
And on thy weary Shoulders bring it back.
While, groaning under this laborious Life,
They insolently call thee *Hector*'s Wife;
Upbraid thy *Bondage* with thy Husband's name;
And from my Glory propagate thy Shame.
This when they say, thy Sorrows will encrease
With anxious thoughts of former Happiness;
That he is dead who cou'd thy wrongs redress.
But I opprest with Iron Sleep before,
Shall hear thy unavailing Cries no more.

He said.
Then, holding forth his *Arms*, he took his *Boy*,
(The Pledge of Love, and other hope of *Troy*;)
The fearful Infant turn'd his Head away;
And on his Nurse's Neck reclining lay,
His unknown Father shunning with affright,
And looking back on so uncouth a sight.
Daunted to see a Face with Steel o're-spread,
And his high Plume, that nodded o're his Head.
His Sire and Mother smil'd with silent Joy;
And *Hector* hasten'd to relieve his *Boy*;
Dismiss'd his burnish'd Helm, that shone afar,
(The Pride of Warriours, and the Pomp of War:)
Th' *Illustrious Babe*, thus reconcil'd, he took:
Hugg'd in his *Arms*, and kiss'd, and thus he spoke.

Parent of Gods, and Men, propitious *Jove*,
And you bright Synod of the Pow'rs above;
On this my Son your Gracious Gifts bestow;
Grant him to live, and great in *Arms* to grow:
To Reign in *Troy*; to Govern with Renown:
To shield the People, and assert the Crown:
That, when hereafter he from War shall come,
And bring his *Trojans* Peace and Triumph home,
Some aged Man, who lives this act to see,
And who in former times remember'd me,
May say the Son in Fortitude and Fame
Out-goes the Mark; and drowns his Father's Name:
That at these words his Mother may rejoice:
And add her Suffrage to the publick Voice.

Thus having said,
He first with suppliant Hands the Gods ador'd:
Then to the Mother's *Arms* the Child restor'd:
With Tears and Smiles she took her Son, and press'd
Th' Illustrious Infant to her fragrant *Breast*.
He wiping her fair Eyes, indulg'd her Grief,
And eas'd her Sorrows with this last Relief.

My Wife and Mistress, drive thy fears away;
Nor give so bad an Omen to the Day:
Think not it lies in any *Grecian*'s Pow'r,
To take my Life before the fatal Hour.
When that arrives, nor good nor bad can fly
Th' irrevocable Doom of Destiny.
Return, and to divert thy thoughts at home,
There task thy Maids, and exercise the Loom,
Employ'd in Works that Womankind become.
The Toils of War, and Feats of Chivalry
Belong to Men, and most of all to me.
At this, for new Replies he did not stay,
But lac'd his Crested Helm, and strode away:

   His lovely Consort to her House return'd:
And looking often back in silence mourn'd:
Home when she came, her secret Woe she vents,
And fills the Palace with her loud Laments:
Those loud Laments her ecchoing Maids restore,
And *Hector*, yet alive, as dead deplore.

Daphnis
From Theocritus Idyll 27

Daphnis.	The Shepheard *Paris* bore the *Spartan* Bride
	By force away, and then by force enjoy'd;
	But I by free consent can boast a Bliss,
	A fairer *Helen*, and a sweeter kiss.
Chloris.	Kisses are empty joyes and soon are o're.
Daph.	A Kiss betwixt the lips is something more.
Chlo.	I wipe my mouth, and where's your kissing then?
Daph.	I swear you wipe it to be kiss'd agen.
Chlo.	Go tend your Herd, and kiss your Cows at home;
	I am a Maid, and in my Beauties bloom.
Daph.	'Tis well remember'd, do not waste your time;
	But wisely use it e're you pass your prime.
Chlo.	Blown Roses hold their sweetness to the last,
	And Raisins keep their luscious native taste.
Daph.	The Sun's too hot; those Olive shades are near;
	I fain wou'd whisper something in your ear.
Chlo.	'Tis honest talking where we may be seen,
	God knows what secret mischief you may mean;
	I doubt you'l play the Wag and kiss agen.
Daph.	At least beneath yon' Elm you need not fear;
	My Pipe's in tune, if you'r dispos'd to hear.
Chlo.	Play by your self, I dare not venture thither:
	You, and your naughty Pipe go hang together.
Daph.	Coy Nymph beware, lest *Venus* you offend:
Chlo.	I shall have chaste *Diana* still to friend.
Daph.	You have a Soul, and *Cupid* has a Dart;
Chlo.	*Diana* will defend, or heal my heart.
	Nay, fie what mean you in this open place;
	Unhand me, or, I sware, I'le scratch your face.
	Let go for shame; you make me mad for spight;

	My mouth's my own; and if you kiss I'le bite.
Daph.	Away with your dissembling Female tricks:
	What, wou'd you 'scape the fate of all your Sex?
Chlo.	I swear I'le keep my Maidenhead till death,
	And die as pure as Queen *Elizabeth*.
Daph.	Nay mum for that; but let me lay thee down;
	Better with me, than with some nauseous Clown.
Chlo.	I'de have you know, if I were so inclin'd.
	I have bin wo'd by many a wealthy Hind;
	But never found a Husband to my mind.
Daph.	But they are absent all; and I am here;
Chlo.	The matrimonial Yoke is hard to bear;
	And Marriage is a woful word to hear.
Daph.	A scar Crow, set to frighten fools away;
	Marriage has joys; and you shall have a say.
Chlo.	Sour sawce is often mix'd with our delight,
	You kick by day more than you kiss by night.
Daph.	Sham stories all; but say the worst you can,
	A very Wife fears neither God nor Man.
Chlo.	But Child-birth is they say, a deadly pain;
	It costs at least a Month to knit again.
Daph.	*Diana* cures the wounds *Lucina* made;
	Your Goddess is a Midwife by her Trade.
Chlo.	But I shall spoil my Beauty if I bear.
Daph.	But Mam and Dad are pretty names to hear.
Chlo.	But there's a Civil question us'd of late;
	Where lies my jointure, where your own Estate?
Daph.	My Flocks, my Fields, my Wood, my Pastures take,
	With settlement as good as Law can make.
Chlo.	Swear then you will not leave me on the common,
	But marry me, and make an honest Woman.
Daph.	I swear by *Pan* (tho' he wears horns you'll say)
	Cudgell'd and kick'd, I'le not be forc'd away.
Chlo.	I bargain for a wedding Bed at least,
	A house, and handsome Lodging for a guest.
Daph.	A house well furnish'd shall be thine to keep;

	And for a flock-bed I can sheer my Sheep.
Chlo	What Tale shall I to my old Father tell?
Daph.	'T will make him Chuckle thou'rt bestow'd so well.
Chlo.	But after all, in troth I am to blame
	To be so loving, e're I know your Name.
	A pleasant sounding name's a pretty thing:
Daph.	Faith, mine's a very pretty name to sing;
	They call me *Daphnis*: *Lycidas* my Syre,
	Both sound as well as Woman can desire.
	Nomæa bore me; Farmers in degree,
	He a good Husband, a good Houswife she.
Chlo.	Your kindred is not much amiss, 'tis true,
	Yet I am somewhat better born than you.
Daph.	I know your Father, and his Family;
	And without boasting am as good as he
	Menaleas; and no Master goes before.
Chlo.	Hang both our Pedigrees; not one word more;
	But if you love me let me see your Living,
	Your House and Home; for seeing is believing.
Daph.	See first yon *Cypress* Grove, (a shade from noon;)
Chlo.	Browze on my goats; for I'le be with you soon.
Daph.	Feed well my Bulls, to whet your appetite;
	That each may take a lusty Leap at Night.
Chlo.	What do you mean (uncivil as you are,)
	To touch my breasts, and leave my bosome bare?
Daph.	These pretty bubbies first I make my own.
Chlo.	Pull out your hand, I swear, or I shall swoon.
Daph.	Why does thy ebbing blood forsake thy face?
Chlo.	Throw me at least upon a cleaner place:
	My Linnen ruffled, and my Wastcoat soyling,
	What, do you think new Cloaths, were made for spoyling?
Daph.	I'le lay my Lambskins underneath thy back:
Chlo.	My Head Geer's off; what filthy work you make!
Daph.	To *Venus* first, I lay these off'rings by;
Chlo.	Nay first look round, that no body be nigh:

	Methinks I hear a whisp'ring in the Grove.
Daph.	The *Cypress* Trees are telling Tales of love.
Chlo.	You tear off all behind me, and before me;
	And I'm as naked as my Mother bore me.
Daph.	I'le buy thee better Cloaths than these I tear,
	And lie so close, I'le cover thee from Air.
Chlo.	Y'are liberal now; but when your turn is sped,
	You'l wish me choak'd with every crust of Bread.
Daph.	I'le give thee more, much more than I have told;
	Wou'd I cou'd coyn my very heart to Gold.
Chlo.	Forgive thy handmaid (Huntress of the wood,)
	I see there's no resisting flesh and blood!
Daph.	The noble deed is done; my Herds I'le cull;
	Cupid, be thine a Calf; and *Venus*, thine a Bull.
Chlo.	A Maid I came, in an unlucky hour,
	But hence return, without my Virgin flour.
Daph.	A Maid is but a barren Name at best;
	If thou canst hold, I bid for twins at least.

    Thus did this happy Pair their love dispence
With mutual joys, and gratifi'd their sense;
The God of Love was there a bidden Guest;
And present at his own Mysterious Feast.
His azure Mantle underneath he spred,
And scatter'd Roses on the Nuptial Bed;
While folded in each others arms they lay,
He blew the flames, and furnish'd out the play,
And from their Foreheads wip'd the balmy sweat
    away.
First rose the Maid, and with a glowing Face,
Her down cast eyes beheld her print upon the grass;
Thence to her Herd she sped her self in haste:
The Bridegroom started from his Trance at last,
And pipeing homeward jocoundly he past.

from De Rerum Natura

from The beginning of the First Book

Delight of Humane kind, and Gods above;
Parent of *Rome*; Propitious Queen of Love;
Whose vital pow'r, Air, Earth, and Sea supplies;
And breeds what e'r is born beneath the rowling Skies:
For every kind, by thy prolifique might,
Springs, and beholds the Regions of the light:
Thee, Goddess thee, the clouds and tempests fear,
And at thy pleasing presence disappear:
For thee the Land in fragrant Flow'rs is drest,
For thee the Ocean smiles, and smooths her wavy breast;
And Heav'n it self with more serene, and purer light is blest.
For when the rising Spring adorns the Mead,
And a new Scene of Nature stands display'd,
When teeming Budds, and chearful greens appear,
And Western gales unlock the lazy year,
The joyous Birds thy welcome first express,
Whose native Songs thy genial fire confess:
Then salvage Beasts bound o're their slighted food,
Strook with thy darts, and tempt the raging floud:
All Nature is thy Gift; Earth, Air, and Sea:
Of all that breaths, the various progeny,
Stung with delight, is goaded on by thee.
O're barren Mountains, o're the flow'ry Plain,
The leavy Forest, and the liquid Main
Extends thy uncontroul'd and boundless reign.
Through all the living Regions dost thou move,
And scatter'st, where thou goest, the kindly seeds of Love:
Since then the race of every living thing,
Obeys thy pow'r; since nothing new can spring

Without thy warmth, without thy influence bear,
Or beautiful, or lovesome can appear,
Be thou my ayd: My tuneful Song inspire,
And kindle with thy own productive fire.

from Against the Fear of Death

What has this Bugbear death to frighten Man,
If Souls can die, as well as Bodies can?
For, as before our Birth we felt no pain
When Punique arms infested Land and Mayn,
When Heav'n and Earth were in confusion hurl'd
For the debated Empire of the World,
Which aw'd with dreadful expectation lay,
Sure to be Slaves, uncertain who shou'd sway:
So, when our mortal frame shall be disjoyn'd,
The lifeless Lump, uncoupled from the mind,
From sense of grief and pain we shall be free;
We shall not feel, because we shall not Be.
Though Earth in Seas, and Seas in Heav'n were lost,
We shou'd not move, we only shou'd be tost.
Nay, ev'n suppose when we have suffer'd Fate,
The Soul cou'd feel in her divided state,
What's that to us, for we are only we
While Souls and bodies in one frame agree?
Nay, tho' our Atoms shou'd revolve by chance,
And matter leape into the former dance;
Tho' time our Life and motion cou'd restore,
And make our Bodies what they were before,
What gain to us wou'd all this bustle bring,
The new made man wou'd be another thing;
When once an interrupting pause is made,
That individual Being is decay'd.

*

And therefore if a Man bemoan his lot,
That after death his mouldring limbs shall rot,
Or flames, or jaws of Beasts devour his Mass,
Know he's an unsincere, unthinking Ass.
A secret Sting remains within his mind,
The fool is to his own cast offals kind;
He boasts no sense can after death remain, ⎫
Yet makes himself a part of life again: ⎬
As if some other He could feel the pain. ⎭
If, while he live, this thought molest his head,
What Wolf or Vulture shall devour me dead,
He wasts his days in idle grief, nor can
Distinguish 'twixt the Body and the Man:
But thinks himself can still himself survive;
And what when dead he feels not, feels alive.
Then he repines that he was born to die,
Nor knows in death there is no other He,
No living He remains his grief to vent,
And o're his senseless Carcass to lament.
If after death 'tis painful to be torn
By Birds and Beasts, then why not so to burn,
Or drench'd in floods of honey to be soak'd,
Imbalm'd to be at once preserv'd and choak'd;
Or on an ayery Mountains top to lie
Expos'd to cold and Heav'ns inclemency,
Or crowded in a Tomb to be opprest
With Monumental Marble on thy breast?
But to be snatch'd from all thy household joys,
From thy Chast Wife, and thy dear prattling boys,
Whose little arms about thy Legs are cast
And climbing for a Kiss prevent their Mothers hast,
Inspiring secret pleasure thro' thy Breast,
All these shall be no more: thy Friends opprest,
Thy Care and Courage now no more shall free:
Ah Wretch, thou cry'st, ah! miserable me,
One woful day sweeps children, friends, and wife,

And all the brittle blessings of my life!
Add one thing more, and all thou say'st is true;
Thy want and wish of them is vanish'd too,
Which well consider'd were a quick relief,
To all thy vain imaginary grief.
For thou shalt sleep and never wake again,
And quitting life, shall quit thy living pain.
But we thy friends shall all those sorrows find,
Which in forgetful death thou leav'st behind,
No time shall dry our tears, nor drive thee from our mind.

*

All things, like thee, have time to rise and rot;
And from each others ruin are begot;
For life is not confin'd to him or thee;
'Tis giv'n to all for use; to none for Property.
Consider former Ages past and gone,
Whose Circles ended long e're thine begun,
Then tell me Fool, what part in them thou hast?
Thus may'st thou judge the future by the past.
What horrour seest thou in that quiet state,
What Bugbear dreams to fright thee after Fate?
No Ghost, no Gobblins, that still passage keep,
But all is there serene, in that eternal sleep.
For all the dismal Tales that Poets tell,
Are verify'd on Earth, and not in Hell.
No *Tantalus* looks up with fearful eye,
Or dreads th' impending Rock to crush him from on high:
But fear of Chance on earth disturbs our easie hours:
Or vain imagin'd wrath, of vain imagin'd Pow'rs.
No *Tityus* torn by Vultures lies in Hell;
Nor cou'd the Lobes of his rank liver swell
To that prodigious Mass for their eternal meal.
Not tho' his monstrous bulk had cover'd o're
Nine spreading Acres, or nine thousand more;
Not tho' the Globe of earth had been the Gyants floor.

Nor in eternal torments cou'd he lie;
Nor cou'd his Corps sufficient food supply.
But he's the *Tityus*, who by Love opprest,
Or Tyrant Passion preying on his breast,
And ever anxious thoughts, is robb'd of rest.
The *Sisiphus* is he, whom noise and strife
Seduce from all the soft retreats of life,
To vex the Government, disturb the Laws;
Drunk with the Fumes of popular applause,
He courts the giddy Crowd to make him great,
And sweats and toils in vain, to mount the sovereign Seat.
For still to aim at pow'r, and still to fail,
Ever to strive and never to prevail,
What is it, but in reasons true account
To heave the Stone against the rising Mount;
Which urg'd, and labour'd, and forc'd up with pain,
Recoils and rowls impetuous down, and smoaks along the plain.

*

Mean time, when thoughts of death disturb thy head;
Consider, *Ancus* great and good is dead;
Ancus thy better far, was born to die,
And thou, dost thou bewail mortality?
So many Monarchs with their mighty State,
Who rul'd the World, were overrul'd by fate.
That haughty King, who Lorded o're the Main,
And whose stupendous Bridge did the wild Waves restrain,
(In vain they foam'd, in vain they threatned wreck,
While his proud Legions march'd upon their back:)
Him death, a greater Monarch, overcame;
Nor spared his guards the more, for their immortal name.
The *Roman* chief, the *Carthaginian* dread, ⎫
Scipio the Thunder Bolt of War is dead, ⎬
And like a common Slave, by fate in triumph led. ⎭
The Founders of invented Arts are lost;
And Wits who made Eternity their boast;

Where now is *Homer* who possest the Throne?
Th' immortal Work remains, the mortal Author's gone.
Democritus perceiving age invade,
His Body weakn'd, and his mind decay'd,
Obey'd the summons with a chearful face;
Made hast to welcome death, and met him half the race.
That stroke, ev'n *Epicurus* cou'd not bar,
Though he in Wit surpass'd Mankind, as far
As does the midday Sun, the midnight Star.
And thou, dost thou disdain to yield thy breath,
Whose very life is little more than death?
More than one half by Lazy sleep possest; –
And when awake, thy Soul but nods at best,
Day-Dreams and sickly thoughts revolving in thy breast.
Eternal troubles haunt thy anxious mind,
Whose cause and cure thou never hop'st to find;
But still uncertain, with thy self at strife,
Thou wander'st in the *Labyrinth* of Life.

from Concerning the Nature of Love

Nature for meat, and drink provides a space;
And when receiv'd they fill their certain place;
Hence thirst and hunger may be satisfi'd,
But this repletion is to Love deny'd:
Form, feature, colour, whatsoe're delight
Provokes the Lovers endless appetite,
These fill no space, nor can we thence remove
With lips, or hands, or all our instruments of love:
In our deluded grasp we nothing find,
But thin aerial shapes, that fleet before the mind.
As he who in a dream with drought is curst,
And finds no real drink to quench his thirst,
Runs to imagin'd Lakes his heat to steep,
And vainly swills and labours in his sleep;
So Love with fantomes cheats our longing eyes,

77

Which hourly seeing never satisfies;
Our hands pull nothing from the parts they strain,
But wander o're the lovely limbs in vain:
Nor when the Youthful pair more clossely joyn,
When hands in hands they lock, and thighs in thighs they twine;
Just in the raging foam of full desire,
When both press on, both murmur, both expire,
They gripe, they squeeze, their humid tongues they dart,
As each wou'd force their way to t'others heart:
In vain; they only cruze about the coast,
For bodies cannot pierce, nor be in bodies lost:
As sure they strive to be, when both engage,
In that tumultuous momentary rage,
So 'tangled in the Nets of Love they lie,
Till Man dissolves in that excess of joy.
Then, when the gather'd bag has burst its way,
And ebbing tydes the slacken'd nerves betray,
A pause ensues; and Nature nods a while,
Till with recruited rage new Spirits boil;
And then the same vain violence returns,
With flames renew'd th' erected furnace burns.
Agen they in each other wou'd be lost,
But still by adamantine bars are crost;
All wayes they try, successeless all they prove,
To cure the secret sore of lingring love.

FROM THE LATIN OF VIRGIL

from The Georgics

[In Praise of Italy]

But neither *Median* Woods, (a plenteous Land,)
Fair *Ganges*, *Hermus* rolling Golden Sand,
Nor *Bactria*, nor the richer *Indian* Fields,
Nor all the Gummy Stores *Arabia* yields;
Nor any foreign Earth of greater Name,
Can with sweet *Italy* contend in Fame.
No Bulls, whose Nostrils breath a living Flame,
Have turn'd our Turf, no Teeth of Serpents here
Were sown, an armed Host, and Iron Crop to bear.
But fruitful Vines, and the fat Olives fraight,
And Harvests heavy with their fruitful weight,
Adorn our Fields; and on the chearful Green,
The grazing Flocks and lowing Herds are seen.
The Warrior Horse, here bred, is taught to train,
There flows *Clitumnus* thro' the flow'ry Plain;
Whose Waves, for Triumphs after prosp'rous War,
The Victim Ox, and snowy Sheep prepare.
Perpetual Spring our happy Climate sees,
Twice breed the Cattle, and twice bear the Trees;
And Summer Suns recede by slow degrees.

Our Land is from the Rage of Tygers freed,
Nor nourishes the Lyon's angry Seed;
Nor pois'nous Aconite is here produc'd,
Or grows unknown, or is, when known, refus'd.
Nor in so vast a length our Serpents glide,
Or rais'd on such a spiry Volume ride.

Next add our Cities of Illustrious Name,
Their costly Labour and stupend'ous Frame:
Our Forts on steepy Hills, that far below

79

See wanton Streams, in winding Valleys flow.
Our twofold Seas, that washing either side,
A rich Recruit of Foreign Stores provide.

[Spring]

The Spring adorns the Woods, renews the Leaves;
The Womb of Earth the genial Seed receives.
For then Almighty *Jove* descends, and pours
Into his buxom Bride his fruitful Show'rs.
And mixing his large Limbs with hers, he feeds
Her Births with kindly Juice, and fosters teeming Seeds.
Then joyous Birds frequent the lonely Grove,
And Beasts, by Nature stung, renew their Love.
Then Fields the Blades of bury'd Corn disclose,
And while the balmy Western Spirit blows,
Earth to the Breath her Bosom dares expose.
With kindly Moisture then the Plants abound,
The Grass securely springs above the Ground;
The tender Twig shoots upward to the Skies,
And on the Faith of the new Sun relies.
The swerving Vines on the tall Elms prevail,
Unhurt by Southern Show'rs or Northern Hail.
They spread their Gems the genial Warmth to share:
And boldly trust their Buds in open Air.
In this soft Season (Let me dare to sing,)
The World was hatch'd by Heav'ns Imperial King:
In prime of all the Year, and Holydays of Spring.

[Happy the Man]

Happy the Man, who, studying Nature's Laws,
Thro' known Effects can trace the secret Cause.
His Mind possessing, in a quiet state,
Fearless of Fortune, and resign'd to Fate.
And happy too is he, who decks the Bow'rs
Of Sylvans, and adores the Rural Pow'rs:

Whose Mind, unmov'd, the Bribes of Courts can see;
Their glitt'ring Baits, and Purple Slavery.
Nor hopes the People's Praise, nor fears their Frown, ⎫
Nor, when contending Kindred tear the Crown, ⎬
Will set up one, or pull another down. ⎭

  Without Concern he hears, but hears from far,
Of Tumults and Descents, and distant War:
Nor with a Superstitious Fear is aw'd,
For what befals at home, or what abroad.
Nor envies he the Rich their heapy Store,
Nor his own Peace disturbs, with Pity for the Poor.
He feeds on Fruits, which, of their own accord,
The willing Ground, and laden Trees afford.
From his lov'd Home no Lucre him can draw; ⎫
The Senates mad Decrees he never saw; ⎬
Nor heard, at bawling Bars, corrupted Law. ⎭
Some to the Seas, and some to Camps resort,
And some with Impudence invade the Court.
In foreign Countries others seek Renown,
With Wars and Taxes others waste their own.
And Houses burn, and houshold Gods deface,
To drink in Bowls which glitt'ring Gems enchase:
To loll on Couches, rich with *Cytron* Steds,
And lay their guilty Limbs in *Tyrian* Beds.
This Wretch in Earth intombs his Golden Ore,
Hov'ring and brooding on his bury'd Store.
Some Patriot Fools to pop'lar Praise aspire,
Or Publick Speeches, which worse Fools admire.
While from both Benches, with redoubl'd Sounds,
Th' Applause of Lords and Commoners abounds.
Some through Ambition, or thro' Thirst of Gold;
Have slain their Brothers, or their Country sold:
And leaving their sweet Homes, in Exile run
To Lands that lye beneath another Sun.

[The Joys of Sweet Coition]

Thus every Creature, and of every Kind,
The secret Joys of sweet Coition find:
Not only Man's Imperial Race; but they
That wing the liquid Air, or swim the Sea,
Or haunt the Desart, rush into the flame:
For Love is Lord of all; and is in all the same.
'Tis with this rage, the Mother Lion stung,
Scours o're the Plain; regardless of her young:
Demanding Rites of Love, she sternly stalks;
And hunts her Lover in his lonely Walks.
Tis then the shapeless Bear his Den forsakes;
In Woods and Fields a wild destruction makes.
Boars whet their Tusks; to battel Tygers move;
Enrag'd with hunger, more enrag'd with love.
Then wo to him, that in the desart Land
Of *Lybia* travels, o're the burning Sand.
The Stallion snuffs the well-known Scent afar;
And snorts and trembles for the distant Mare:
Nor Bitts nor Bridles, can his rage restrain;
And rugged Rocks are interpos'd in vain:
He makes his way o're Mountains, and contemns
Unruly Torrents, and unfoorded Streams.
The bristled Boar, who feels the pleasing wound,
New grinds his arming Tusks, and digs the ground.
The sleepy Leacher shuts his little Eyes;
About his churning Chaps the frothy bubbles rise:
He rubs his sides against a Tree; prepares
And hardens both his Shoulders for the Wars ...
I pass the Wars that spotted *Linx's* make
With their fierce Rivals, for the Females sake:
The howling Wolves, the Mastiffs amorous rage;
When ev'n the fearful Stag dares for his Hind engage.
But far above the rest, the furious Mare,
Barr'd from the Male, is frantick with despair.

For when her pouting Vent declares her pain,
She tears the Harness, and she rends the Rein;
For this; (when *Venus* gave them rage and pow'r)
Their Masters mangl'd Members they devour;
Of Love defrauded in their longing Hour.
For Love they force through Thickets of the Wood,
They climb the steepy Hills, and stem the Flood.

When at the Spring's approach their Marrow burns,
(For with the Spring their Genial Warmth returns)
The Mares to Cliffs of rugged Rocks repair,
And with wide Nostrils snuff the Western Air:
When (wondrous to relate) the Parent Wind,
Without the Stallion, propagates the Kind.
Then fir'd with amorous rage, they take their flight
Through Plains, and mount the Hills unequal height;
Nor to the North, nor to the Rising Sun,
Nor Southward to the Rainy Regions run,
But boring to the West, and hov'ring there
With gaping Mouths, they draw prolifick air:
With which impregnate, from their Groins they shed
A slimy Juice, by false Conception bred.
The Shepherd knows it well; and calls by Name
Hippomanes, to note the Mothers Flame.
This, gather'd in the Planetary Hour,
With noxious Weeds, and spell'd with words of pow'r,
Dire Stepdames in the Magick Bowl infuse;
And mix, for deadly draughts, the poys'nous juice.

from The Aeneid

'Arms, and the Man I sing'

Arms, and the Man I sing, who, forc'd by Fate,
And haughty *Juno*'s unrelenting Hate;
Expell'd and exil'd, left the *Trojan* Shoar:
Long Labours, both by Sea and Land he bore;
And in the doubtful War, before he won
The *Latian* Realm, and built the destin'd Town:
His banish'd Gods restor'd to Rites Divine,
And setl'd sure Succession in his Line:
From whence the Race of *Alban* Fathers come,
And the long Glories of Majestick *Rome*.
   O Muse! the Causes and the Crimes relate,
What Goddess was provok'd, and whence her hate:
For what Offence the Queen of Heav'n began
To persecute so brave, so just a Man!
Involv'd his anxious Life in endless Cares,
Expos'd to Wants, and hurry'd into Wars!
Can Heav'nly Minds such high resentment show;
Or exercise their Spight in Human Woe?

[The Building of Carthage]

The Prince, with Wonder, sees the stately Tow'rs,
Which late were Huts, and Shepherds homely Bow'rs;
The Gates and Streets; and hears, from ev'ry part,
The Noise, and buisy Concourse of the Mart.
The toiling *Tyrians* on each other call,
To ply their Labour. Some extend the Wall,
Some build the Citadel; the brawny Throng,
Or dig, or push unweildy Stones along.
Some for their Dwelling chuse a Spot of Ground,
Which, first design'd, with Ditches they surround.
Some Laws ordain, and some attend the Choice

Of holy Senates, and elect by Voice.
Here some design a Mole, while others there
Lay deep Foundations for a Theatre:
From Marble Quarries mighty Columns hew,
For Ornaments of Scenes, and future view.
Such is their Toyl, and such their buisy Pains,
As exercise the Bees in flow'ry Plains;
When Winter past, and Summer scarce begun,
Invites them forth to labour in the Sun:
Some lead their Youth abroad, while some condense
Their liquid Store, and some in Cells dispence.
Some at the Gate stand ready to receive
The Golden Burthen, and their Friends relieve.
All, with united Force, combine to drive
The lazy Drones from the laborious Hive;
With Envy stung, they view each others Deeds;
The fragrant Work with Diligence proceeds.

[The Ghost of Hector Appears to Aeneas]

'Twas in the dead of Night, when Sleep repairs
Our Bodies worn with Toils, our Minds with Cares,
When *Hector*'s Ghost before my sight appears:
A bloody Shrowd he seem'd, and bath'd in Tears.
Such as he was, when, by *Pelides* slain,
Thessalian Coursers drag'd him o're the Plain.
Swoln were his Feet, as when the Thongs were thrust
Through the bor'd holes, his Body black with dust.
Unlike that *Hector*, who return'd from toils
Of War Triumphant, in *Æacian* Spoils:
Or him, who made the fainting *Greeks* retire,
And lanch'd against their Navy *Phrygian* Fire.
His Hair and Beard stood stiffen'd with his gore;
And all the Wounds he for his Country bore,
Now stream'd afresh, and with new Purple ran:
I wept to see the visionary Man ...

[The Killing of Priam, King of Troy]

Where e're the raging Fire had left a space,
The *Grecians* enter, and possess the Place.
  Perhaps you may of *Priam*'s Fate enquire.
He, when he saw his Regal Town on fire,
His ruin'd Palace, and his ent'ring Foes,
On ev'ry side inevitable woes;
In Arms, disus'd, invests his Limbs decay'd
Like them, with Age; a late and useless aid.
His feeble shoulders scarce the weight sustain: ⎫
Loaded, not arm'd, he creeps along, with pain; ⎬
Despairing of Success; ambitious to be slain! ⎭
Uncover'd but by Heav'n, there stood in view
An Altar; near the hearth a Lawrel grew;
Dodder'd with Age, whose Boughs encompass round
The Household Gods, and shade the holy Ground.
Here *Hecuba*, with all her helpless Train
Of Dames, for shelter sought, but sought in vain.
Driv'n like a Flock of Doves along the skie,
Their Images they hugg, and to their Altars fly.
The Queen, when she beheld her trembling Lord,
And hanging by his side a heavy Sword,
What Rage, she cry'd, has seiz'd my Husband's mind;
What Arms are these, and to what use design'd?
These times want other aids: were *Hector* here,
Ev'n *Hector* now in vain, like *Priam* wou'd appear.
With us, one common shelter thou shalt find,
Or in one common Fate with us be join'd.
She said, and with a last Salute embrac'd
The poor old Man, and by the Lawrel plac'd.
Behold *Polites*, one of *Priam*'s Sons,
Pursu'd by *Pyrrhus*, there for safety runs.
Thro Swords, and Foes, amaz'd and hurt, he flies
Through empty Courts, and open Galleries:
Him *Pyrrhus*, urging with his Lance, pursues;

And often reaches, and his thrusts renews.
The Youth transfix'd, with lamentable Cries
Expires, before his wretched Parent's Eyes.
Whom, gasping at his feet, when *Priam* saw,
The Fear of Death gave place to Nature's Law.
And shaking more with Anger, than with Age,
The Gods, said He, requite thy brutal Rage:
As sure they will, Barbarian, sure they must,
If there be Gods in Heav'n, and Gods be just:
Who tak'st in Wrongs an insolent delight;
With a Son's death t' infect a Father's sight.
Not He, whom thou and lying Fame conspire
To call thee his; Not He, thy vaunted Sire,
Thus us'd my wretched Age: The Gods he fear'd,
The Laws of Nature and of Nations heard.
He chear'd my Sorrows, and for Sums of Gold
The bloodless Carcass of my *Hector* sold.
Pity'd the Woes a Parent underwent,
And sent me back in safety from his Tent.

   This said, his feeble hand a Javelin threw,
Which flutt'ring, seem'd to loiter as it flew:
Just, and but barely, to the Mark it held,
And faintly tinckl'd on the Brazen Shield.

   Then *Pyrrhus* thus: go thou from me to Fate;
And to my Father my foul deeds relate.
Now dye: with that he dragg'd the trembling Sire,
Slidd'ring through clotter'd Blood, and holy Mire,
(The mingl'd Paste his murder'd Son had made,)
Haul'd from beneath the violated Shade;
And on the Sacred Pile, the Royal Victim laid.
His right Hand held his bloody Fauchion bare;
His left he twisted in his hoary Hair:
Then, with a speeding Thrust, his Heart he found:
The lukewarm Blood came rushing through the wound,
And sanguine Streams distain'd the sacred Ground.
Thus *Priam* fell: and shar'd one common Fate

With *Troy* in Ashes, and his ruin'd State:
He, who the Scepter of all *Asia* sway'd,
Whom Monarchs like domestick Slaves obey'd.
On the bleak Shoar now lies th' abandon'd King,
*A headless Carcass, and a nameless thing.

[Dido and the Deer]

Sick with desire, and seeking him she loves,
From Street to Street, the raving *Dido* roves.
So when the watchful Shepherd, from the Blind,
Wounds with a random Shaft the careless Hind;
Distracted with her pain she flies the Woods,
Bounds o're the Lawn, and seeks the silent Floods;
With fruitless Care; for still the fatal Dart
Sticks in her side; and ranckles in her Heart.
And now she leads the *Trojan* Chief, along
The lofty Walls, amidst the buisie Throng;
Displays her *Tyrian* Wealth, and rising Town,
Which Love, without his Labour, makes his own.
This Pomp she shows to tempt her wand'ring Guest;
Her falt'ring Tongue forbids to speak the rest.

[Fame]

The loud Report through *Lybian* Cities goes;
Fame, the great Ill, from small beginnings grows.
Swift from the first; and ev'ry Moment brings
New Vigour to her flights, new Pinions to her wings.
Soon grows the Pygmee to Gygantic size;
Her Feet on Earth, her Forehead in the Skies:
Inrag'd against the Gods, revengeful Earth
Produc'd her last of the *Titanian* birth.
Swift is her walk, more swift her winged hast:
A monstrous Fantom, horrible and vast;

* *This whole line is taken from Sir* John Denham. [Dryden's note]

As many Plumes as raise her lofty flight,
So many piercing Eyes inlarge her sight:
Millions of opening Mouths to Fame belong;
And ev'ry Mouth is furnish'd with a Tongue:
And round with listning Ears the flying Plague is hung.
She fills the peaceful Universe with Cries;
No Slumbers ever close her wakeful Eyes.
By Day from lofty Tow'rs her Head she shews;
And spreads through trembling Crowds disastrous News.
With Court Informers haunts, and Royal Spies,
Things done relates, not done she feigns; and mingles Truth
    with Lyes.
Talk is her business; and her chief delight
To tell of Prodigies, and cause affright.

[The Mountain Oak]

As when the Winds their airy Quarrel try;
Justling from ev'ry quarter of the Sky;
This way and that, the Mountain Oak they bend,
His Boughs they shatter, and his Branches rend;
With Leaves, and falling Mast, they spread the Ground,
The hollow Vallies echo to the Sound:
Unmov'd, the Royal Plant their Fury mocks;
Or shaken, clings more closely to the Rocks:
Far as he shoots his tow'ring Head on high,
So deep in Earth his fix'd Foundations lye.
No less a Storm the *Trojan* Heroe bears;
Thick Messages and loud Complaints he hears;
And bandy'd Words, still beating on his Ears.
Sighs, Groans and Tears, proclaim his inward Pains,
But the firm purpose of his Heart remains.

[Charon]

There *Charon* stands, who rules the dreary Coast:
A sordid God; down from his hoary Chin

A length of Beard descends; uncomb'd, unclean:
His Eyes, like hollow Furnaces on Fire:
A Girdle, foul with grease, binds his obscene Attire.
He spreads his Canvas, with his Pole he steers;
The Freights of flitting Ghosts in his thin Bottom bears.
He look'd in Years; yet in his Years were seen
A youthful Vigour, and Autumnal green.
An Airy Crowd came rushing where he stood;
Which fill'd the Margin of the fatal Flood.
Husbands and Wives, Boys and unmarry'd Maids;
And mighty Heroes more Majestick Shades.
And Youths, intomb'd before their Fathers Eyes,
With hollow Groans, and Shrieks, and feeble Cries:
Thick as the Leaves in Autumn strow the Woods:
Or Fowls, by Winter forc'd, forsake the Floods,
And wing their hasty flight to happier Lands: }
Such, and so thick, the shiv'ring Army stands: }
And press for passage with extended hands. }

[Anchises Shows His Son Aeneas the Souls in Limbo]

Now in a secret Vale, the *Trojan* sees }
A sep'rate Grove, thro' which a gentle Breeze }
Plays with a passing Breath, and whispers thro' the Trees. }
And just before the Confines of the Wood,
The gliding *Lethe* leads her silent Flood.
About the Boughs an Airy Nation flew,
Thick as the humming Bees, that hunt the Golden Dew;
In Summer's heat, on tops of Lillies feed,
And creep within their Bells, to suck the balmy Seed.
The winged Army roams the Fields around;
The Rivers and the Rocks remurmur to the sound.
Æneas wond'ring stood: Then ask'd the Cause,
Which to the Stream the Crowding People draws.
Then thus the Sire. The Souls that throng the Flood
Are those, to whom, by Fate, are other Bodies ow'd:

In *Lethe*'s Lake they long Oblivion tast;
Of future Life secure, forgetful of the Past.

[The Death of Pallas]

Then *Turnus*, from his Chariot leaping light,
Address'd himself on Foot to single Fight.
And, as a Lyon; when he spies from far
A Bull, that seems to meditate the War,
Bending his Neck, and spurning back the Sand;
Runs roaring downward from his hilly Stand:
Imagine eager *Turnus* not more slow,
To rush from high on his unequal Foe.
   Young *Pallas*, when he saw the Chief advance
Within due distance of his flying Lance;
Prepares to charge him first: Resolv'd to try
If Fortune wou'd his want of Force supply.
And thus to Heav'n and *Hercules* address'd.
Alcides, once on Earth *Evander*'s Guest,
His Son adjures you by those Holy Rites,
That hospitable Board, those Genial Nights;
Assist my great Attempt to gain this Prize,
And let proud *Turnus* view, with dying Eyes,
His ravish'd Spoils. 'Twas heard, the vain Request;
Alcides mourn'd: And stifled Sighs within his Breast.
Then *Jove*, to sooth his Sorrow, thus began:
Short bounds of Life are set to Mortal Man,
'Tis Vertues work alone to stretch the narrow Span.
So many Sons of Gods in bloody Fight,
Around the Walls of *Troy*, have lost the Light:
My own *Sarpedon* fell beneath his Foe,
Nor I, his mighty Sire, cou'd ward the Blow.
Ev'n *Turnus* shortly shall resign his Breath;
And stands already on the Verge of Death.
This said, the God permits the fatal Fight,
But from the *Latian* Fields averts his sight.

Now with full Force his Spear young *Pallas* threw;
And having thrown, his shining Fauchion drew:
The Steel just graz'd along the Shoulder Joint,
And mark'd it slightly with the glancing Point.
Fierce *Turnus* first to nearer distance drew,
And poiz'd his pointed Spear before he threw:
Then, as the winged Weapon whiz'd along;
See now, said he, whose Arm is better strung.
The Spear kept on the fatal Course, unstay'd
By Plates of Ir'n, which o're the Shield were laid:
Thro' folded Brass, and tough Bull-hides it pass'd,
His Corslet pierc'd, and reach'd his Heart at last.
In vain the Youth tugs at the broken Wood,
The Soul comes issuing with the vital Blood:

[Diomede Refuses an Alliance with the Latians
Against Aeneas]

Attentively he heard us, while we spoke;
Then, with soft Accents, and a pleasing Look,
Made this return. *Ausonian* Race, of old
Renown'd for Peace, and for an Age of Gold,
What Madness has your alter'd Minds possess'd,
To change for War hereditary Rest?
Sollicite Arms unknown, and tempt the Sword,
(A needless Ill your Ancestors abhorr'd?)
We; (for my self I speak, and all the Name
Of *Grecians*, who to *Troy*'s Destruction came;)
Omitting those who were in Battel slain,
Or born by rowling *Simois* to the Main:
Not one but suffer'd, and too dearly bought
The Prize of Honour which in Arms he sought.
Some doom'd to Death, and some in Exile driv'n,
Out-casts, abandon'd by the Care of Heav'n:
So worn, so wretched, so despis'd a Crew,
As ev'n old *Priam* might with Pity view.

Witness the Vessels by *Minerva* toss'd
In Storms, the vengeful *Capharæan* Coast;
Th' *Eubæan* Rocks! The Prince, whose Brother led
Our Armies to revenge his injur'd Bed,
In *Egypt* lost; *Ulysses*, with his Men,
Have seen *Charybdis*, and the *Cyclops* Den:
Why shou'd I name *Idomeneus*, in vain
Restor'd to Scepters, and expell'd again?
Or young *Achilles* by his Rival slain?
Ev'n he, the King of Men, the foremost Name
Of all the *Greeks*, and most renown'd by Fame,
The proud Revenger of another's Wife,
Yet by his own Adult'ress lost his Life:
Fell at his Threshold, and the Spoils of *Troy*,
The foul Polluters of his Bed enjoy.
The Gods have envy'd me the sweets of Life,
My much lov'd Country, and my more lov'd Wife:
Banish'd from both, I mourn; while in the Sky
Transform'd to Birds, my lost Companions fly:
Hov'ring about the Coasts they make their Moan;
And cuff the Cliffs with Pinions not their own.

[Turnus and the Wanton Courser]

Now *Turnus* arms for Fight: His Back and Breast,
Well temper'd Steel, and scaly Brass invest:
The Cuishes, which his brawny Thighs infold,
Are mingled Metal damask'd o're with Gold.
His faithful Fauchion sits upon his side;
Nor Casque, nor Crest, his manly Features hide:
But bare to view, amid surrounding Friends,
With Godlike Grace, he from the Tow'r descends.
Exulting in his Strength, he seems to dare
His absent Rival, and to promise War.
    Freed from his Keepers, thus with broken Reins,
The wanton Courser prances o're the Plains:

Or in the Pride of Youth o'releaps the Mounds;
And snuffs the Females in forbidden Grounds.
Or seeks his wat'ring in the well known Flood,
To quench his Thirst, and cool his fiery Blood:
He swims luxuriant, in the liquid Plain,
And o're his Shoulder flows his waving Mane:
He neighs, he snorts, he bears his Head on high;
Before his ample Chest the frothy Waters fly.

[Camilla, the Amazon]

Mean time, *Latonian Phœbe* from the Skies,
Beheld th' approaching War with hateful Eies.
And call'd the light-foot *Opis*, to her aid,
Her most belov'd, and ever trusty Maid.
Then with a sigh began: *Camilla* goes
To meet her Death, amidst her Fatal Foes.
The Nymph I lov'd of all my Mortal Train;
Invested with *Diana*'s Arms, in vain.
Nor is my kindness for the Virgin, new,
'Twas born with Her, and with her Years it grew:
Her Father *Metabus*, when forc'd away
From old *Privernum*, for Tyrannick sway;
Snatch'd up, and sav'd from his prevailing Foes,
This tender Babe, Companion of his Woes.
Casmilla was her Mother; but he drown'd
One hissing Letter in a softer sound,
And call'd *Camilla*. Thro the Woods, he flies;
Wrap'd in his Robe the Royal Infant lies.
His Foes in sight, he mends his weary pace;
With shouts and clamours they pursue the Chace.
The Banks of *Amasene* at length he gains; ⎫
The raging Flood his farther flight restrains: ⎬
Rais'd o're the Borders with unusual Rains. ⎭
Prepar'd to Plunge into the Stream, He fears:
Not for himself, but for the Charge he bears.

Anxious he stops a while; and thinks in haste;
Then, desp'rate in Distress, resolves at last.
A knotty Lance of well-boil'd Oak he bore;
The middle part with Cork he cover'd o're:
He clos'd the Child within the hollow Space;
With Twigs of bending Osier bound the Case.
Then pois'd the Spear, heavy with Human Weight;
And thus invok'd my Favour for the Freight.
Accept, great Goddess of the Woods, he said,
Sent by her Sire, this dedicated Maid:
Thro' Air she flies a Suppliant to thy Shrine;
And the first Weapons that she knows, are thine.
He said; and with full Force the Spear he threw:
Above the sounding Waves *Camilla* flew.
Then, press'd by Foes, he stemm'd the stormy Tyde;
And gain'd, by stress of Arms, the farther Side.
His fasten'd Spear he pull'd from out the Ground;
And, Victor of his Vows, his Infant Nymph unbound.
Nor after that, in Towns which Walls inclose,
Wou'd trust his hunted Life amidst his Foes.
But rough, in open Air he chose to lye:
Earth was his Couch, his Cov'ring was the Sky.
On Hills unshorn, or in a desart Den,
He shunn'd the dire Society of Men.
A Shepherd's solitary Life he led:
His Daughter with the Milk of Mares he fed;
The Dugs of Bears, and ev'ry Salvage Beast,
He drew, and thro' her Lips the Liquor press'd.
The little *Amazon* cou'd scarcely go,
He loads her with a Quiver and a Bow:
And, that she might her stagg'ring Steps command,
He with a slender Jav'lin fills her Hand:
Her flowing Hair no golden Fillet bound;
Nor swept her trayling Robe the dusty Ground.
Instead of these, a Tyger's Hide o'respread
Her Back and Shoulders, fasten'd to her Head.

The flying Dart she first attempts to fling;
And round her tender Temples toss'd the Sling:
Then, as her Strength with Years increas'd, began
To pierce aloft in Air the soaring Swan:
And from the Clouds to fetch the Heron and the Crane.
The *Tuscan* Matrons with each other vy'd,
To bless their Rival Sons with such a Bride:
But she disdains their Love; to share with me
The Silvan Shades, and vow'd Virginity.

[The Death of Turnus and the End of the Poem]

And as, when heavy Sleep has clos'd the sight,
The sickly Fancy labours in the Night:
We seem to run; and destitute of Force
Our sinking Limbs forsake us in the Course:
In vain we heave for Breath; in vain we cry:
The Nerves unbrac'd, their usual Strength deny;
And, on the Tongue the falt'ring Accents dye:
So *Turnus* far'd: what ever means he try'd,
All force of Arms, and points of Art employ'd,
The Fury flew athwart; and made th' Endeavour void.

   A thousand various Thoughts his Soul confound:
He star'd about; nor Aid nor Issue found:
His own Men stop the Pass; and his own Walls surround.
Once more he pauses; and looks out again:
And seeks the Goddess Charioteer in vain.
Trembling he views the Thund'ring Chief advance:
And brandishing aloft the deadly Lance:
Amaz'd he cow'rs beneath his conqu'ring Foe,
Forgets to ward; and waits the coming Blow.
Astonish'd while he stands, and fix'd with Fear,
Aim'd at his Shield he sees th' impending Spear.

   The Heroe measur'd first, with narrow view,
The destin'd Mark: And rising as he threw,
With its full swing the fatal Weapon flew.

Not with less Rage the rattling Thunder falls;
Or Stones from batt'ring Engins break the Walls:
Swift as a Whirlwind, from an Arm so strong,
The Lance drove on; and bore the Death along.
Nought cou'd his sev'n-fold Shield the Prince avail,
Nor ought beneath his Arms the Coat of Mail;
It pierc'd thro' all; and with a grizly Wound,
Transfix'd his Thigh, and doubled him to Ground.
With Groans the *Latins* rend the vaulted Sky:
Woods, Hills, and Valleys, to the Voice reply.

  Now low on Earth the lofty Chief is laid;
With Eyes cast upward, and with Arms display'd;
And Recreant thus to the proud Victor pray'd.
I know my Death deserv'd, nor hope to live:
Use what the Gods, and thy good Fortune give.

  Yet think; oh think, if Mercy may be shown,
(Thou hadst a Father once; and hast a Son:)
Pity my Sire, now sinking to the Grave;
And for *Anchises* sake, old *Daunus* save!
Or, if thy vow'd Revenge pursue my Death;
Give to my Friends my Body void of Breath!
The *Latian* Chiefs have seen me beg my Life;
Thine is the Conquest, thine the Royal Wife:
Against a yielded Man, 'tis mean ignoble Strife.

  In deep Suspence the *Trojan* seem'd to stand;
And just prepar'd to strike repress'd his Hand.
He rowl'd his Eyes, and ev'ry Moment felt
His manly Soul with more Compassion melt.
When, casting down a casual Glance, he spy'd
The Golden Belt that glitter'd on his side:
The fatal Spoils which haughty *Turnus* tore
From dying *Pallas*, and in Triumph wore.
Then rowz'd anew to Wrath, he loudly cries,
(Flames, while he spoke, came flashing from his Eyes:)
Traytor, dost thou, dost thou to Grace pretend,
Clad, as thou art, in Trophees of my Friend?

To his sad Soul a grateful Off'ring go;
'Tis *Pallas*, *Pallas* gives this deadly Blow.
He rais'd his Arm aloft; and at the Word,
Deep in his Bosom drove the shining Sword.
The streaming Blood distain'd his Arms around:
And the disdainful Soul came rushing thro' the Wound.

Odes, Book I, 9

Behold yon' Mountains hoary height
   Made higher with new Mounts of Snow;
Again behold the Winters weight
   Oppress the lab'ring Woods below:
And streams with Icy fetters bound,
Benum'd and crampt to solid ground.

With well heap'd Logs dissolve the cold,
   And feed the genial hearth with fires;
Produce the Wine, that makes us bold,
   And sprightly Wit and Love inspires:
For what hereafter shall betide,
God, if 'tis worth his care, provide.

Let him alone with what he made,
   To toss and turn the World below;
At his command the storms invade;
   The winds by his Commission blow
Till with a Nod he bids 'em cease,
And then the Calm returns, and all is peace.

To morrow and her works defie,
   Lay hold upon the present hour,
And snatch the pleasures passing by,
   To put them out of Fortunes pow'r:
Nor love, nor love's delights disdain,
What e're thou get'st to day is gain.

Secure those golden early joyes,
   That Youth unsowr'd with sorrow bears,
E're with'ring time the taste destroyes,
   With sickness and unwieldy years!
For active sports, for pleasing rest,

This is the time to be possest;
The best is but in season best.

The pointed hour of promis'd bliss,
    The pleasing whisper in the dark,
The half unwilling willing kiss,
    The laugh that guides thee to the mark,
When the kind Nymph wou'd coyness feign,
And hides but to be found again,
These, these are joyes the Gods for Youth ordain.

Odes, Book III, 29
Paraphras'd in Pindarique Verse

I

Descended of an ancient Line,
   That long the *Tuscan* Scepter sway'd,
Make haste to meet the generous wine,
   Whose piercing is for thee delay'd:
The rosie wreath is ready made;
   And artful hands prepare
The fragrant *Syrian* Oyl, that shall perfume thy hair.

II

When the Wine sparkles from a far,
   And the well-natur'd Friend cries, come away;
Make haste, and leave thy business and thy care,
   No mortal int'rest can be worth thy stay.

III

Leave for a while thy costly Country Seat;
   And, to be Great indeed, forget
The nauseous pleasures of the Great:
      Make haste and come:
Come and forsake thy cloying store;
   Thy Turret that surveys, from high,
The smoke, and wealth, and noise of *Rome*;
   And all the busie pageantry
That wise men scorn, and fools adore:
Come, give thy Soul a loose, and taste the pleasures of the poor.

IV

Sometimes 'tis grateful to the Rich, to try
A short vicissitude, and fit of Poverty:

A savoury Dish, a homely Treat,
Where all is plain, where all is neat,
Without the stately spacious Room,
The *Persian* Carpet, or the *Tyrian* Loom,
Clear up the cloudy foreheads of the Great.

V

The Sun is in the Lion mounted high;
        The *Syrian* Star
        Barks from a far;
And with his sultry breath infects the Sky;
The ground below is parch'd, the heav'ns above us fry.
        The Shepheard drives his fainting Flock,
        Beneath the covert of a Rock;
        And seeks refreshing Rivulets nigh:
        The *Sylvans* to their shades retire,
Those very shades and streams, new shades and streams require;
And want a cooling breeze of wind to fan the rageing fire.

VI

Thou, what befits the new Lord May'r,
And what the City Faction dare,
And what the *Gallique* Arms will do,
And what the Quiver bearing Foe,
Art anxiously inquisitive to know:
But God has, wisely, hid from humane sight
        The dark decrees of future fate;
        And sown their seeds in depth of night;
    He laughs at all the giddy turns of State;
When Mortals search too soon, and fear too late.

VII

Enjoy the present smiling hour;
And put it out of Fortunes pow'r:

The tide of bus'ness, like the running stream,
    Is sometimes high, and sometimes low,
A quiet ebb, or a tempestuous flow,
        And alwayes in extream.
    Now with a noiseless gentle course
    It keeps within the middle Bed;
    Anon it lifts aloft the head,
And bears down all before it, with impetuous force:
    And trunks of Trees come rowling down,
    Sheep and their Folds together drown:
Both House and Homested into Seas are borne,
And Rocks are from their old foundations torn,
And woods made thin with winds, their scatter'd honours mourn.

VIII

    Happy the Man, and happy he alone,
    He, who can call to day his own:
    He, who secure within, can say
To morrow do thy worst, for I have liv'd to day.
    Be fair, or foul, or rain, or shine,
The joys I have possest, in spight of fate are mine.
    Not Heav'n it self upon the past has pow'r;
But what has been, has been, and I have had my hour.

IX

    Fortune, that with malicious joy,
        Does Man her slave oppress,
    Proud of her Office to destroy,
        Is seldome pleas'd to bless.
    Still various and unconstant still;
But with an inclination to be ill;
    Promotes, degrades, delights in strife,
    And makes a Lottery of life.
    I can enjoy her while she's kind;
    But when she dances in the wind,

And shakes her wings, and will not stay,
        I puff the Prostitute away:
The little or the much she gave, is quietly resign'd:
    Content with poverty, my Soul, I arm;
    And Vertue, tho' in rags, will keep me warm.

x

        What is't to me,
Who never sail in her unfaithful Sea,
    If Storms arise, and Clouds grow black;
    If the Mast split and threaten wreck.
    Then let the greedy Merchant fear
            For his ill gotten gain;
    And pray to Gods that will not hear,
While the debating winds and billows bear
            His Wealth into the Main.
    For me secure from Fortunes blows,
    (Secure of what I cannot lose,)
    In my small Pinnace I can sail,
            Contemning all the blustring roar;
                And running with a merry gale,
    With friendly Stars my safety seek
    Within some little winding Creek;
                And see the storm a shore.

from Epode, 2

How happy in his low degree,
How rich in humble Poverty, is he,
Who leads a quiet country life!
Discharg'd of business, void of strife,
And from the gripeing Scrivener free.
(Thus e're the Seeds of Vice were sown,
   Liv'd Men in better Ages born,
Who Plow'd with Oxen of their own
   Their small paternal field of Corn.)
Nor Trumpets summon him to War
   Nor drums disturb his morning Sleep,
Nor knows he Merchants gainful care,
   Nor fears the dangers of the deep.
The clamours of contentious Law,
   And Court and state he wisely shuns,
Nor brib'd with hopes nor dar'd with awe
   To servile Salutations runs:
But either to the clasping Vine
   Does the supporting Poplar Wed,
Or with his pruneing hook disjoyn
   Unbearing Branches from their Head,
   And grafts more happy in their stead:
Or climbing to a hilly Steep
   He views his Herds in Vales afar
Or Sheers his overburden'd Sheep,
   Or mead for cooling drink prepares,
   Of Virgin honey in the Jars.
Or in the now declining year
   When bounteous *Autumn* rears his head,
He joyes to pull the ripen'd Pear,
   And clustring Grapes with purple spread.
The fairest of this his fruit he serves,
   Priapus thy rewards:

Sylvanus too his part deserves,
    Whose care the fences guards.
Sometimes beneath an ancient Oak,
    Or on the matted grass he lies;
No God of Sleep he need invoke,
    The stream that o're the pebbles flies
    With gentle slumber crowns his Eyes.
The Wind that Whistles through the sprays
    Maintains the consort of the Song;
And hidden Birds with native layes
    The golden sleep prolong.
But when the blast of Winter blows,
    And hoary frost inverts the year,
Into the naked Woods he goes
    And seeks the tusky Boar to rear,
    With well mouth'd hounds and pointed Spear.
Or spreads his subtile Nets from sight
    With twinckling glasses to betray
The Larkes that in the Meshes light,
    Or makes the fearful Hare his prey.
Amidst his harmless easie joys
    No anxious care invades his health,
Nor Love his peace of mind destroys,
    Nor wicked avarice of Wealth.
But if a chast and pleasing Wife,
To ease the business of his Life,
Divides with him his houshold care,
Such as the *Sabine* Matrons were,
Such as the swift *Apulians* Bride,
    Sunburnt and Swarthy tho' she be,
Will fire for Winter Nights provide,
    And without noise will oversee,
    His Children and his Family,
And order all things till he come,
Sweaty and overlabour'd, home;
If she in pens his Flocks will fold,

And then produce her Dairy store,
With Wine to drive away the cold,
    And unbought dainties of the poor;
Not Oysters of the *Lucrine* Lake
    My sober appetite wou'd wish,
    Nor *Turbet*, or the Foreign Fish
That rowling Tempests overtake,
    And hither waft the costly dish.
Not *Heathpout*, or the rarer Bird,
    Which *Phasis*, or *Ionia* yields,
More pleasing morsels wou'd afford
    Than the fat Olives of my fields;
Than Shards or Mallows for the pot,
    That keep the loosen'd Body sound,
Or than the Lamb that falls by Lot,
    To the just Guardian of my ground.
Amidst these feasts of happy Swains,
    The jolly Shepheard smiles to see
His flock returning from the Plains;
    The Farmer is as pleas'd as he
To view his Oxen, sweating smoak,
Bear on their Necks the loosen'd Yoke.
To look upon his menial Crew,
    That sit around his cheerful hearth,
And bodies spent in toil renew
    With wholesome Food and Country Mirth.
This *Morecraft* said within himself;
    Resolv'd to leave the wicked Town,
    And live retir'd upon his own;
He call'd his Mony in:
    But the prevailing love of pelf,
    Soon split him on the former shelf,
And put it out again.

Amores, Book I, Elegy IV

To his Mistress, whose Husband is invited to a Feast
with them. The Poet instructs her how to behave her self
in his Company.

Your Husband will be with us at the Treat;
May that be the last Supper he shall Eat.
And am poor I, a Guest invited there,
Only to see, while he may touch the Fair?
To see you Kiss and Hug your nauseous Lord,
While his leud Hand descends below the Board?
Now wonder not that *Hippodamia*'s Charms,
At such a sight, the Centaurs urg'd to Arms:
That in a rage, they threw their Cups aside,
Assail'd the Bridegroom, and wou'd force the Bride.
I am not half a Horse, (I wish I were:)
Yet hardly can from you my Hands forbear.
Take, then, my Counsel; which, observ'd, may be
Of some Importance both to you and me.
Be sure to come before your Man be there,
There's nothing can be done, but come howe're.
Sit next him, (that belongs to Decency;)
But tread upon my Foot in passing by.
Read in my Looks what silently they speak,
And slily, with your Eyes, your Answer make.
My lifted Eye-brow shall declare my Pain,
My Right-Hand to his fellow shall complain.
And on the Back a Letter shall design;
Besides a Note that shall be Writ in Wine.
When e're you think upon our last Embrace,
With your Fore-finger gently touch your Face.
If any Word of mine offend my Dear,
Pull, with your Hand, the Velvet of your Ear.

If you are pleas'd with what I do or say,
Handle your Rings, or with your Fingers play.
As Suppliants use at Altars, hold the Boord
When e're you wish the Devil may take your Lord.
When he fills for you, never touch the Cup;
But bid th' officious Cuckold drink it up.
The Waiter on those Services employ;
Drink you, and I will snatch it from the Boy:
Watching the part where your sweet Mouth has been,
And thence, with eager Lips, will suck it in.
If he, with Clownish Manners thinks it fit
To taste, and offers you the nasty Bit,
Reject his greazy Kindness, and restore
Th' unsav'ry Morsel he had chew'd before.
Nor let his Arms embrace your Neck, nor rest
Your tender Cheek upon his hairy Brest.
Let not his Hand within your Bosom stray,
And rudely with your pretty Bubbies play.
But, above all, let him no Kiss receive;
That's an Offence I never can forgive.
Do not, O do not that sweet Mouth resign,
Lest I rise up in Arms; and cry 'Tis mine.
I shall thrust in betwixt, and void of Fear
The manifest Adult'rer will appear.
These things are plain to sight, but more I doubt
What you conceal beneath your Petticoat.
Take not his Leg between your tender Thighs,
Nor, with your Hand, provoke my Foe to rise.
How many Love-Inventions I deplore,
Which I, my self, have practis'd all before?
How oft have I been forc'd the Robe to lift
In Company; to make a homely shift
For a bare Bout, ill huddled o're in hast,
While o're my Side the Fair her Mantle cast.
You to your Husband shall not be so kind;
But, lest you shou'd, your Mantle leave behind.

Encourage him to Tope, but Kiss him not,
Nor mix one drop of Water in his Pot.
If he be Fuddled well, and Snores apace,
Then we may take Advice from Time and Place.
When all depart, while Complements are loud,
Be sure to mix among the thickest Crowd:
There I will be, and there we cannot miss,
Perhaps to Grubble, or at least to Kiss.
Alas, what length of Labour I employ,
Just to secure a short and transient Joy!
For Night must part us; and when Night is come,
Tuck'd underneath his Arms he leads you Home.
He locks you in, I follow to the Door,
His Fortune envy, and my own deplore.
He kisses you, he more than kisses too;
Th' outrageous Cuckold thinks it all his due.
But, add not to his Joy, by your Consent;
And let it not be giv'n, but only lent:
Return no Kiss, nor move in any sort;
Make it a dull, and a malignant Sport.
Had I my Wish, he shou'd no Pleasure take,
But slubber o're your Business for my sake.
And what e're Fortune shall this Night befal,
Coakes me to morrow, by foreswearing all.

from Metamorphoses, Book I

[Jove Looses the South Wind and Neptune the Floods]

The Northern breath, that freezes Floods, he binds;
With all the race of Cloud-dispelling Winds:
The South he loos'd, who Night and Horror brings;
And Foggs are shaken from his flaggy Wings.
From his divided Beard, two Streams he pours,
His head and rhumy eyes, distill in showers.
With Rain his Robe and heavy Mantle flow;
And lazy mists, are lowring on his brow:
Still as he swept along, with his clench't fist
He squeez'd the Clouds, th' imprison'd Clouds resist:
The Skies from Pole to Pole, with peals resound;
And show'rs inlarg'd, come pouring on the ground.
Then, clad in Colours of a various dye,
Junonian Iris, breeds a new supply;
To feed the Clouds: Impetuous Rain descends;
The bearded Corn, beneath the Burden bends:
Defrauded Clowns, deplore their perish'd grain;
And the long labours of the Year are vain.

*

The Floods, by Nature Enemies to Land,
And proudly swelling with their new Command,
Remove the living Stones, that stopt their way,
And gushing from their Source, augment the Sea.
Then, with his Mace, their Monarch struck the Ground:
With inward trembling, Earth receiv'd the wound;
And rising streams a ready passage found.
Th' expanded Waters gather on the Plain:
They flote the Fields, and over-top the Grain;
Then rushing onwards, with a sweepy sway,
Bear Flocks and Folds, and lab'ring Hinds away.

Nor safe their Dwelling were, for, sap'd by Floods,
Their Houses fell upon their Household Gods.
The solid Piles, too strongly built to fall,
High o're their Heads, behold a watry Wall:
Now Seas and Earth were in confusion lost;
A World of Waters, and without a Coast.

One climbs a Cliff; one in his Boat is born;
And Ploughs above, where late he sow'd his Corn.
Others o're Chimney tops and Turrets row,
And drop their Anchors, on the Meads below:
Or downward driv'n, they bruise the tender Vine,
Or tost aloft, are knock't against a Pine.
And where of late, the Kids had cropt the Grass,
The Monsters of the deep, now take their place.
Insulting Nereids on the Cities ride,
And wondring Dolphins o're the Palace glide.
On leaves and masts of mighty Oaks they brouze;
And their broad Finns, entangle in the Boughs,
The frighted Wolf, now swims amongst the Sheep;
The yellow Lyon wanders in the deep:
His rapid force, no longer helps the Boar:
The Stag swims faster, than he ran before.
The Fowls, long beating on their Wings in vain,
Despair of Land, and drop into the Main.
Now Hills and Vales, no more distinction know;
And levell'd Nature, lies oppress'd below.
The most of Mortals perish in the Flood:
The small remainder dies for want of Food.

[Deucalion and Pyrrha Renew Creation
by Casting Stones Behind Them]

The Stones (a Miracle to Mortal View,
But long Tradition makes it pass for true)
Did first the Rigour of their Kind expell,
And, suppl'd into softness, as they fell,

Then swell'd, and swelling, by degrees grew warm;
And took the Rudiments of Humane Form.
Imperfect shapes: in Marble such are seen
When the rude Chizzel does the Man begin;
While yet the roughness of the Stone remains,
Without the rising Muscles, and the Veins.
The sappy parts, and next resembling juice,
Were turn'd to moisture, for the Bodies use:
Supplying humours, blood, and nourishment;
The rest, (too solid to receive a bent;)
Converts to bones; and what was once a vein
Its former Name, and Nature did retain.
By help of Pow'r Divine, in little space   ⎫
What the Man threw, assum'd a Manly face;   ⎬
And what the Wife, renew'd the Female Race. ⎭
Hence we derive our Nature; born to bear
Laborious life; and harden'd into care.

    The rest of Animals, from teeming Earth
Produc'd, in various forms receiv'd their birth.
The native moisture, in its close retreat,
Digested by the Sun's Ætherial heat,
As in a kindly Womb, began to breed:
Then swell'd, and quicken'd by the vital seed.
And some in less, and some in longer space,
Were ripen'd into form, and took a several face.
Thus when the *Nile* from *Pharian* Fields is fled,
And seeks with Ebbing Tides, his ancient Bed,
The fat Manure, with Heav'nly Fire is warm'd;
And crusted Creatures, as in Wombs are form'd;
Those, when they turn the Glebe, the Peasants find;
Some rude; and yet unfinish'd in their Kind:
Short of their Limbs, a lame imperfect Birth;
One half alive; and one of lifeless Earth.

    For heat and moisture, when in Bodies joyn'd,
The temper that results from either Kind
Conception makes; and fighting till they mix,

Their mingl'd Atoms in each other fix.
Thus Nature's hand, the Genial Bed prepares,
With Friendly Discord, and with fruitful Wars.
   From hence the surface of the Ground, with Mud
And Slime besmear'd, (the faeces of the Flood)
Receiv'd the Rays of Heav'n; and sucking in
The Seeds of Heat, new Creatures did begin:
Some were of sev'ral sorts produc'd before,
But of new Monsters, Earth created more.

from Baucis and Philemon
Out of the Eighth Book of Ovid's Metamorphoses

Then *Lelex* rose, an old experienc'd Man,
And thus with sober Gravity began:
Heav'ns Pow'r is Infinite: Earth, Air, and Sea,
The Manufacture Mass, the making Pow'r obey:
By Proof to clear your Doubt; In *Phrygian* Ground
Two neighb'ring Trees, with Walls encompass'd round,
Stand on a mod'rate Rise, with wonder shown,
One a hard Oak, a softer Linden one:
I saw the Place and them, by *Pittheus* sent
To *Phrygian* Realms, my Grandsire's Government.
Not far from thence is seen a Lake, the Haunt
Of Coots, and of the fishing Cormorant:
Here *Jove* with *Hermes* came; but in Disguise
Of mortal Men conceal'd their Deities;
One laid aside his thunder, one his Rod;
And many toilsom Steps together trod:
For Harbour at a thousand Doors they knock'd,
Not one of all the thousand but was lock'd.
At last an hospitable House they found,
A homely Shed; the Roof, not far from Ground,
Was thatch'd with Reeds, and Straw together bound.
There *Baucis* and *Philemon* liv'd, and there
Had liv'd long marry'd, and a happy Pair:
Now old in Love, though little was their Store,
Inur'd to Want, their Poverty they bore,
Nor aim'd at Wealth, professing to be poor.
For Master or for Servant here to call,
Was all alike, where only Two were All.
Command was none, where equal Love was paid,
Or rather both commanded, both obey'd.
　　From lofty Roofs the Gods repuls'd before,
Now stooping, enter'd through the little Door:

The Man (their hearty Welcome first express'd)
A common Settle drew for either Guest,
Inviting each his weary Limbs to rest.
But e'er they sat, officious *Baucis* lays
Two Cushions stuff'd with Straw, the Seat to raise;
Course, but the best she had; then rakes the Load
Of Ashes from the Hearth, and spreads abroad
The living Coals; and, lest they shou'd expire,
With Leaves and Barks she feeds her Infant-fire:
It smoaks; and then with trembling Breath she blows,
Till in a chearful Blaze the Flames arose.
With Brush-wood and with Chips she strengthens these,
And adds at last the Boughs of rotten Trees.
The Fire thus form'd, she sets the Kettle on,
(Like burnish'd Gold the little Seether shone)
Next took the Coleworts which her Husband got
From his own Ground, (a small well-water'd Spot;)
She stripp'd the Stalks of all their Leaves; the best
She cull'd, and then with handy-care she dress'd.
High o'er the Hearth a Chine of Bacon hung;
Good old *Philemon* seiz'd it with a Prong,
And from the sooty Rafter drew it down,
Then cut a Slice, but scarce enough for one;
Yet a large Portion of a little Store,
Which for their Sakes alone he wish'd were more.
This in the Pot he plung'd without delay,
To tame the Flesh, and drain the Salt away.
The Time between, before the Fire they sat,
And shorten'd the Delay by pleasing Chat.

A Beam there was, on which a Beechen Pail
Hung by the Handle, on a driven Nail:
This fill'd with Water, gently warm'd, they set
Before their Guests; in this they bath'd their Feet,
And after with clean Towels dry'd their Sweat:

This done, the Host produc'd the genial Bed,
Sallow the Feet, the Borders, and the Sted,
Which with no costly Coverlet they spread;
But course old Garments, yet such Robes as these
They laid alone, at Feasts, on Holydays.
The good old Huswife tucking up her Gown,
The Table sets; th' invited Gods lie down.
The Trivet-Table of a Foot was lame,
A Blot which prudent *Baucis* overcame,
Who thrusts beneath the limping Leg, a Sherd,
So was the mended Board exactly rear'd:
Then rubb'd it o'er with newly-gather'd Mint,
A wholesom Herb, that breath'd a grateful Scent.
Pallas began the Feast, where first was seen
The party-colour'd Olive, Black, and Green:
Autumnal Cornels next in order serv'd,
In Lees of Wine well pickl'd, and preserv'd.
A Garden-Sallad was the third Supply,
Of Endive, Radishes, and Succory:
Then Curds and Cream, the Flow'r of Country-Fare,
And new-laid Eggs, which *Baucis* busie Care
Turn'd by a gentle Fire, and roasted rear.
All these in Earthen Ware were serv'd to Board;
And next in place, an Earthen Pitcher stor'd
With Liquor of the best the Cottage cou'd afford.
This was the Tables Ornament, and Pride,
With Figures wrought: Like Pages at his Side
Stood Beechen Bowls; and these were shining clean,
Vernish'd with Wax without, and lin'd within.
By this the boiling Kettle had prepar'd,
And to the Table sent the smoaking Lard;
On which with eager Appetite they dine,
A sav'ry Bit, that serv'd to rellish Wine;
The Wine it self was suiting to the rest,
Still working in the Must, and lately press'd.
The Second Course succeeds like that before,

Plums, Apples, Nuts, and of their Wintry Store,
Dry Figs, and Grapes, and wrinkl'd Dates were set
In Canisters, t' enlarge the little Treat:
All these a Milk-white Honey-comb surround,
Which in the midst the Country-Banquet crown'd:
But the kind Hosts their Entertainment grace
With hearty Welcom, and an open Face:
In all they did, you might discern with ease,
A willing Mind, and a Desire to please.

Mean time the Beechen Bowls went round, and still
Though often empty'd, were observ'd to fill;
Fill'd without Hands, and of their own accord
Ran without Feet, and danc'd about the Board.
Devotion seiz'd the Pair, to see the Feast
With Wine, and of no common Grape, increas'd;
And up they held their Hands, and fell to Pray'r,
Excusing as they cou'd, their Country Fare.

One Goose they had, ('twas all they cou'd allow)
A wakeful Cent'ry, and on Duty now,
Whom to the Gods for Sacrifice they vow:
Her, with malicious Zeal, the Couple view'd;
She ran for Life, and limping they pursu'd:
Full well the fowl perceiv'd their bad intent,
And wou'd not make her Masters Compliment;
But persecuted, to the Pow'rs she flies,
And close between the Legs of *Jove* she lies:
He with a gracious Ear the Suppliant heard,
And sav'd her Life; then what he was declar'd,
And own'd the God. The Neighbourhood, said he,
Shall justly perish for Impiety:
You stand alone exempted; but obey
With speed, and follow where we lead the way:
Leave these accurs'd; and to the Mountains Height
Ascend; nor once look backward in your Flight.

They haste, and what their tardy Feet deny'd,
The trusty Staff (their better Leg) supply'd.

An Arrows Flight they wanted to the Top,
And there secure, but spent with Travel, stop;
Then turn their now no more forbidden Eyes;
Lost in a Lake the floated Level lies:
A Watry Desart covers all the Plains,
Their Cot alone, as in an Isle, remains:
Wondring with weeping Eyes, while they deplore
Their Neighbours Fate, and Country now no more,
Their little Shed, scarce large enough for Two,
Seems, from the Ground increas'd, in Height and Bulk to grow.
A stately Temple shoots within the Skies,
The Crotches of their Cot in Columns rise:
The Pavement polish'd Marble they behold,
The Gates with Sculpture grac'd, the Spires and Tiles of Gold.
  Then thus the Sire of Gods, with Look serene,
Speak thy Desire, thou only Just of Men;
And thou, O Woman, only worthy found
To be with such a Man in Marriage bound.
  A while they whisper; then to *Jove* address'd,
Philemon thus prefers their joint Request.
We crave to serve before your sacred Shrine,
And offer at your Altars Rites Divine:
And since not any Action of our Life
Has been polluted with Domestick Strife,
We beg one Hour of Death; that neither she
With Widows Tears may live to bury me,
Nor weeping I, with wither'd Arms may bear
My breathless *Baucis* to the Sepulcher.
  The Godheads sign their Suit. They run their Race
In the same Tenor all th' appointed Space:
Then, when their Hour was come, while they relate
These past Adventures at the Temple-gate,
Old *Baucis* is by old *Philemon* seen
Sprouting with sudden Leaves of spritely Green:
Old *Baucis* look'd where old *Philemon* stood,
And saw his lengthen'd Arms a sprouting Wood:

New Roots their fasten'd Feet begin to bind,
Their Bodies stiffen in a rising Rind:
Then e'er the Bark above their Shoulders grew,
They give and take at once their last Adieu:
At once, Farewell, O faithful Spouse, they said;
At once th' incroaching Rinds their closing Lips invade.
Ev'n yet, an ancient *Tyanæan* shows
A spreading Oak, that near a Linden grows;
The Neighbourhood confirm the Prodigie,
Grave Men, not vain of Tongue, or like to lie.
I saw my self the Garlands on their Boughs,
And Tablets hung for Gifts of granted Vows;
And off'ring fresher up, with pious Pray'r,
The Good, said I, are God's peculiar Care,
And such as honour Heav'n, shall heav'nly Honour share.

from Ceyx and Alcyone

[Iris Descends to the Cave of Sleep]

Near the *Cymmerians*, in his dark Abode
Deep in a Cavern, dwells the drowzy God;
Whose gloomy Mansion nor the rising Sun
Nor setting, visits, nor the lightsome Noon:
But lazy Vapors round the Region fly,
Perpetual Twilight, and a doubtful Sky;
No crowing Cock does there his Wings display
Nor with his horny Bill provoke the Day;
Nor watchful Dogs, nor the more wakeful Geese,
Disturb with nightly Noise the sacred Peace:
Nor Beast of Nature, nor the Tame are nigh,
Nor Trees with Tempests rock'd, nor human Cry,
But safe Repose without an air of Breath
Dwells here, and a dumb Quiet next to Death.

An Arm of *Lethe* with a gentle flow
Arising upwards from the Rock below,
The Palace moats, and o'er the Pebbles creeps
And with soft Murmurs calls the coming Sleeps:
Around its Entry nodding Poppies grow,
And all cool Simples that sweet Rest bestow;
Night from the Plants their sleepy Virtue drains,
And passing sheds it on the silent Plains:
No Door there was th' unguarded House to keep,
On creaking Hinges turn'd, to break his Sleep.

But in the gloomy Court was rais'd a Bed
Stuff'd with black Plumes, and on an Ebon-sted:
Black was the Cov'ring too, where lay the God
And slept supine, his Limbs display'd abroad:
About his Head fantastick Visions fly,
Which various Images of Things supply,
And mock their Forms, the Leaves on Trees not more;

Nor bearded Ears in Fields, nor Sands upon the Shore.
   The Virgin entring bright indulg'd the Day
To the brown Cave, and brush'd the Dreams away:
The God disturb'd with this new glare of Light
Cast sudden on his Face, unseal'd his Sight,
And rais'd his tardy Head, which sunk agen,
And sinking on his Bosom knock'd his Chin;
At length shook off himself; and ask'd the Dame,
(And asking yawn'd) for what intent she came?

from Cinyras and Myrrha
  Out of the Tenth Book of Ovid's Metamorphoses

[Myrrha's Reflections on Incest]

Ye Gods, ye sacred Laws, my Soul defend
From such a Crime, as all Mankind detest,
And never lodg'd before in Humane Breast!
But is it Sin? Or makes my Mind alone
Th' imagin'd Sin? For Nature makes it none.
What Tyrant then these envious Laws began,
Made not for any other Beast, but Man!
The Father-Bull his Daughter may bestride,
The Horse may make his Mother-Mare a Bride;
What Piety forbids the lusty Ram
Or more salacious Goat, to rut their Dam?
The Hen is free to wed the Chick she bore,
And make a Husband, whom she hatch'd before.
All Creatures else are of a happier Kind,
Whom nor ill-natur'd Laws from Pleasure bind,
Nor Thoughts of Sin disturb their Peace of mind.
But Man, a Slave of his own making lives;
The Fool denies himself what Nature gives:
Too busie Senates, with an over-care
To make us better than our Kind can bear,
Have dash'd a Spice of Envy in the Laws,
And straining up too high, have spoil'd the Cause.
Yet some wise Nations break their cruél Chains,
And own no Laws, but those which Love ordains:
Where happy Daughters with their Sires are join'd,
And Piety is doubly paid in Kind.
O that I had been born in such a Clime,
Not here, where 'tis the Country makes the Crime!
But whither wou'd my impious Fancy stray?
Hence Hopes, and ye forbidden Thoughts away!

His Worth deserves to kindle my Desires,
But with the Love, that Daughters bear to Sires.
Then had not *Cinyras* my Father been,
What hinder'd *Myrrha*'s Hopes to be his Queen?
But the Perverseness of my Fate is such,
That he's not mine, because he's mine too much:
Our Kindred-Blood debars a better Tie;
He might be nearer, were he not so nigh.
Eyes and their Objects never must unite,
Some Distance is requir'd to help the Sight:
Fain wou'd I travel to some Foreign Shore,
Never to see my Native Country more,
So might I to my self my self restore;
So might my Mind these impious Thoughts remove,
And ceasing to behold, might cease to love.

Of the Pythagorean Philosophy
from Ovid's Metamorphoses, Book XV

This let me further add, that Nature knows
No stedfast Station, but, or Ebbs, or Flows:
Ever in motion; she destroys her old,
And casts new Figures in another Mold.
Ev'n Times are in perpetual Flux; and run
Like Rivers from their Fountain rowling on;
For Time no more than Streams, is at a stay:
The flying Hour is ever on her way;
And as the Fountain still supplies her store,
The Wave behind impels the Wave before;
Thus in successive Course the Minutes run,
And urge their Predecessor Minutes on,
Still moving, ever new: For former Things
Are set aside, like abdicated Kings:
And every moment alters what is done,
And innovates some Act till then unknown.

*

Perceiv'st thou not the process of the Year,
How the four Seasons in four Forms appear,
Resembling human Life in ev'ry Shape they wear?
Spring first, like Infancy, shoots out her Head,
With milky Juice requiring to be fed:
Helpless, tho' fresh, and wanting to be led.
The green Stem grows in Stature and in Size,
But only feeds with hope the Farmer's Eyes;
Then laughs the childish Year with Flourets crown'd,
And lavishly perfumes the Fields around,
But no substantial Nourishment receives,
Infirm the Stalks, unsolid are the Leaves.
Proceeding onward whence the Year began
The Summer grows adult, and ripens into Man.

This Season, as in Men, is most repleat,
With kindly Moisture, and prolifick Heat.
Autumn succeeds, a sober tepid age,
Not froze with Fear, nor boiling into Rage;
More than mature, and tending to decay,
When our brown Locks repine to mix with odious Grey.
    Last Winter creeps along with tardy pace,
Sour is his Front, and furrow'd is his Face;
His Scalp if not dishonour'd quite of Hair,
The ragged Fleece is thin, and thin is worse than bare.

*

    Time was, when we were sow'd, and just began
From some few fruitful Drops, the promise of a Man;
Then Nature's Hand (fermented as it was)
Moulded to Shape the soft, coagulated Mass;
And when the little Man was fully form'd,
The breathless Embryo with a Spirit warm'd;
But when the Mothers Throws begin to come,
The Creature, pent within the narrow Room,
Breaks his blind Prison, pushing to repair
His stiffled Breath, and draw the living Air;
Cast on the Margin of the World he lies,
A helpless Babe, but by Instinct he cries.
He next essays to walk, but downward press'd
On four Feet imitates his Brother Beast:
By slow degrees he gathers from the Ground
His Legs, and to the rowling Chair is bound;
Then walks alone; a Horseman now become
He rides a Stick, and travels round the Room:
In time he vaunts among his youthful Peers,
Strong-bon'd, and strung with Nerves, in pride of Years,
He runs with Mettle his first merry Stage,
Maintains the next abated of his Rage,
But manages his Strength, and spares his Age.
Heavy the third, and stiff, he sinks apace,

And tho' 'tis down-hill all, but creeps along the Race.
Now sapless on the verge of Death he stands,
Contemplating his former Feet, and Hands;
And *Milo*-like, his slacken'd Sinews sees,
And wither'd Arms, once fit to cope with *Hercules*, }
Unable now to shake much less to tear the Trees. }

*

All Things are alter'd, nothing is destroy'd,
The shifted Scene, for some new Show employ'd.
    Then to be born, is to begin to be
Some other Thing we were not formerly:
And what we call to Die, is not t' appear,
Or be the Thing that formerly we were.
Those very Elements which we partake,
Alive, when Dead some other Bodies make:
Translated grow, have Sense, or can Discourse,
But Death on deathless Substance has no force.
    That Forms are chang'd I grant; that nothing can
Continue in the Figure it began:
The Golden Age, to Silver was debas'd:
To Copper that; our Mettal came at last.
    The Face of Places, and their Forms decay;
And that is solid Earth, that once was Sea:
Seas in their turn retreating from the Shore,
Make solid Land, what Ocean was before;
And far from Strands are Shells of Fishes found,
And rusty Anchors fix'd on Mountain-Ground:
And what were Fields before, now wash'd and worn
By falling Floods from high, to Valleys turn,
And crumbling still descend to level Lands;
And Lakes, and trembling Bogs are barren Sands:
And the parch'd Desert floats in Streams unknown;
Wondring to drink of Waters not her own.

from Satires, VI

'In Saturn's Reign'

In Saturn's Reign, at Nature's Early Birth,
There was that Thing call'd Chastity on Earth;
When in a narrow Cave, their common shade,
The Sheep the Shepherds and their Gods were laid:
When Reeds and Leaves, and Hides of Beasts were spread
By Mountain Huswifes for their homely Bed,
And Mossy Pillows rais'd, for the rude Husband's head.
Unlike the Niceness of our Modern Dames
(Affected Nymphs with new Affected Names:)
The Cynthia's and the Lesbia's of our Years,
Who for a Sparrow's Death dissolve in Tears.
Those first unpolisht Matrons, Big and Bold,
Gave Suck to Infants of Gygantick Mold;
Rough as their Savage Lords who Rang'd the Wood,
And Fat with Akorns Belcht their windy Food.
For when the World was Bucksom, fresh, and young,
Her Sons were undebauch'd, and therefore strong;
And whether Born in kindly Beds of Earth,
Or strugling from the Teeming Oaks to Birth,
Or from what other Atom they begun,
No Sires they had, or if a Sire the Sun.
Some thin Remains of Chastity appear'd
Ev'n under Jove, but Jove without a Beard:
Before the servile Greeks had learnt to Swear
By Heads of Kings; while yet the Bounteous Year
Her common Fruits in open Plains expos'd,
E're Thieves were fear'd, or Gardens were enclos'd:
At length uneasie Justice upwards flew,
And both the Sisters to the Stars withdrew;

From that Old Æra Whoring did begin,
So Venerably Ancient is the Sin.
Adult'rers next invade the Nuptial State,
And Marriage-Beds creak'd with a Foreign Weight;
All other Ills did Iron times adorn;
But Whores and Silver in one Age were Born.

[Messalina, Wife of the Emperor Claudius]

The good old Sluggard but began to snore,
When from his side up rose th' Imperial Whore:
She who preferr'd the Pleasures of the Night
To Pomps, that are but impotent delight,
Strode from the Palace, with an eager pace,
To cope with a more Masculine Embrace:
Muffl'd she march'd, like Juno in a Clowd,
Of all her Train but one poor Wench allow'd,
One whom in Secret Service she cou'd trust;
The Rival and Companion of her Lust.
To the known Brothel-house she takes her way;
And for a nasty Room gives double pay;
That Room in which the rankest Harlot lay.
Prepar'd for fight, expectingly she lies,
With heaving Breasts, and with desiring Eyes:
Still as one drops, another takes his place,
And baffled still succeeds to like disgrace.
At length, when friendly darkness is expir'd,
And every Strumpet from her Cell retir'd,
She lags behind, and lingring at the Gate,
With a repining Sigh, submits to Fate:
All Filth without and all a Fire within,
Tir'd with the Toyl, unsated with the Sin.
Old Cæsar's Bed the modest Matron seeks;
The steam of Lamps still hanging on her Cheeks

In Ropy Smut; thus foul, and thus bedight,
She brings him back the Product of the Night.

*

There are, who in soft Eunuchs, place their Bliss;
To shun the scrubbing of a Bearded Kiss;
And scape Abortion; but their solid joy
Is when the Page, already past a Boy,
Is Capon'd late; and to the Guelder shown,
With his two Pounders, to Perfection grown.
When all the Navel-string cou'd give, appears;
All but the Beard; and that's the Barber's loss, not theirs.
Seen from afar, and famous for his ware,
He struts into the Bath, among the Fair:
Th' admiring Crew to their Devotions fall;
And, kneeling, on their new Priapus call.
Kerv'd for my Lady's use with her he lies;
And let him drudge for her, if thou art wise;
Rather than trust him with thy Fav'rite Boy;
He proffers Death in proffering to enjoy.

*

She duely, once a Month, renews her Face;
Mean time, it lies in Dawb, and hid in Grease;
Those are the Husband's Nights; she craves her due,
He takes fat Kisses, and is stuck in Glue.
But, to the Lov'd Adult'rer when she steers,
Fresh from the Bath, in brightness she appears:
For him the Rich Arabia sweats her Gum;
And precious Oyls from distant Indies come:
How Haggardly so e're she looks at home.
Th' Eclipse then vanishes; and all her Face
Is open'd, and restor'd to ev'ry Grace.
The Crust remov'd, her Cheeks as smooth as Silk,
Are polish'd with a wash of Asses Milk;
And, shou'd she to the farthest North be sent,

A Train of these attend her Banishment.
But, hadst thou seen her Plaistred up before,
'Twas so unlike a Face, it seem'd a Sore.

from Satires, X

[Sejanus]

Some ask for Envy'd Pow'r; which publick Hate
Pursues, and hurries headlong to their Fate:
Down go the Titles; and the Statue Crown'd,
Is by base Hands in the next River Drown'd.
The Guiltless Horses, and the Chariot Wheel
The same Effects of Vulgar Fury feel:
The Smith prepares his Hammer for the Stroke,
While the Lung'd Bellows hissing Fire provoke;
Sejanus almost first of Roman Names,
The great Sejanus crackles in the Flames:
Form'd in the Forge, the Pliant Brass is laid
On Anvils; and of Head and Limbs are made,
Pans, Cans, and Pispots, a whole Kitchin Trade.
Adorn your Doors with Laurels; and a Bull
Milk white and large, lead to the Capitol;
Sejanus with a Rope, is drag'd along;
The Sport and Laughter of the giddy Throng!
Good Lord, they Cry, what Ethiop Lips he has,
How foul a Snout, and what a hanging Face:
By Heav'n I never cou'd endure his sight;
But say, how came his Monstrous Crimes to Light?
What is the Charge, and who the Evidence
(The Saviour of the Nation and the Prince?)
Nothing of this; but our Old Cæsar sent
A Noisie Letter to his Parliament:
Nay Sirs, if Cæsar writ, I ask no more:
He's Guilty; and the Question's out of Door.
How goes the Mob, (for that's a Mighty thing.)
When the King's Trump, the Mob are for the King:
They follow Fortune, and the Common Cry
Is still against the Rogue Condemn'd to Dye.

from Cymon and Iphigenia

[The Boor Cymon Humanised by Love]

The Fool of Nature, stood with stupid Eyes
And gaping Mouth, that testify'd Surprize,
Fix'd on her Face, nor cou'd remove his Sight,
New as he was to Love, and Novice in Delight:
Long mute he stood, and leaning on his Staff,
His Wonder witness'd with an Ideot laugh;
Then would have spoke, but by his glimmering Sense
First found his want of Words, and fear'd Offence:
Doubted for what he was he should be known,
By his Clown-Accent, and his Country-Tone.
  Through the rude Chaos thus the running Light
Shot the first Ray that pierc'd the Native Night:
Then Day and Darkness in the Mass were mix'd,
Till gather'd in a Globe, the Beams were fix'd:
Last shon the Sun who radiant in his Sphere
Illumin'd Heav'n, and Earth, and rowl'd around the Year.
So Reason in this Brutal Soul began:
Love made him first suspect he was a Man;
Love made him doubt his broad barbarian Sound,
By Love his want of Words, and Wit he found:
That sense of want prepar'd the future way
To Knowledge, and disclos'd the promise of a Day.
  What not his Father's Care, nor Tutor's Art
Cou'd plant with Pains in his unpolish'd Heart,
The best Instructor Love at once inspir'd,
As barren Grounds to Fruitfulness are fir'd:
Love taught him Shame, and Shame with Love at Strife
Soon taught the sweet Civilities of Life;
His gross material Soul at once could find

Somewhat in her excelling all her Kind:
Exciting a Desire till then unknown,
Somewhat unfound, or found in her alone.
This made the first Impression in his Mind,
Above, but just above the Brutal Kind.
For Beasts can like, but not distinguish too,
Nor their own liking by reflection know;
Nor why they like or this, or t'other Face,
Or judge of this or that peculiar Grace,
But love in gross, and stupidly admire;
As Flies allur'd by Light, approach the Fire.
Thus our Man-Beast advancing by degrees
First likes the whole, then sep'rates what he sees;
On sev'ral Parts a sev'ral Praise bestows,
The ruby Lips, the well-proportion'd Nose,
The snowy Skin, the Raven-glossy Hair,
The dimpled Cheek, the Forehead rising fair,
And ev'n in Sleep it self a smiling Air.
From thence his Eyes descending view'd the rest,
Her plump round Arms, white Hands, and heaving Breast.
Long on the last he dwelt, though ev'ry part
A pointed Arrow sped to pierce his Heart.

    Thus in a trice a Judge of Beauty grown,
(A Judge erected from a Country-Clown)
He long'd to see her Eyes in Slumber hid;
And wish'd his own cou'd pierce within the Lid:
He wou'd have wak'd her, but restrain'd his Thought,
And Love new-born the first good Manners taught.

from Palamon and Arcite: or, The Knight's Tale

[Duke Theseus' Speech]

The Cause and Spring of Motion, from above
Hung down on Earth the Golden Chain of Love:
Great was th' Effect, and high was his Intent,
When Peace among the jarring Seeds he sent.
Fire, Flood, and Earth, and Air by this were bound,
And Love, the common Link, the new Creation crown'd.
The Chain still holds; for though the Forms decay,
Eternal Matter never wears away:
The same First Mover certain Bounds has plac'd,
How long those perishable Forms shall last;
Nor can they last beyond the Time assign'd
By that All-seeing, and All-making Mind:
Shorten their Hours they may; for Will is free;
But never pass th' appointed Destiny.
So Men oppress'd, when weary of their Breath,
Throw off the Burden, and subborn their Death.
Then since those Forms begin, and have their End,
On some unalter'd Cause they sure depend:
Parts of the Whole are we; but God the Whole;
Who gives us Life, and animating Soul.
For Nature cannot from a Part derive
That Being, which the Whole can only give:
He perfect, stable; but imperfect We,
Subject to Change, and diff'rent in Degree.
Plants, Beasts, and Man; and as our Organs are,
We more or less of his Perfection share.
But by a long Descent, th' Etherial Fire
Corrupts; and Forms, the mortal Part, expire:
As he withdraws his Vertue, so they pass,

And the same Matter makes another Mass:
This Law th' Omniscient Pow'r was pleas'd to give,
That ev'ry Kind should by Succession live;
That Individuals die, his Will ordains;
The propagated Species still remains.
The Monarch Oak, the Patriarch of the Trees,
Shoots rising up, and spreads by slow Degrees:
Three Centuries he grows, and three he stays,
Supreme in State; and in three more decays:
So wears the paving Pebble in the Street,
And Towns and Tow'rs their fatal Periods meet.
So Rivers, rapid once, now naked lie,
Forsaken of their Springs; and leave their Channels dry.
So Man, at first a Drop, dilates with Heat,
Then form'd, the little Heart begins to beat;
Secret he feeds, unknowing in the Cell;
At length, for Hatching ripe, he breaks the Shell,
And struggles into Breath, and cries for Aid;
Then, helpless, in his Mothers Lap is laid.
He creeps, he walks, and issuing into Man,
Grudges their Life, from whence his own began.
Retchless of Laws, affects to rule alone,
Anxious to reign, and restless on the Throne:
First vegetive, then feels, and reasons last;
Rich of Three Souls, and lives all three to waste.
Some thus; but thousands more in Flow'r of Age:
For few arrive to run the latter Stage.
Sunk in the first, in Battel some are slain,
And others whelm'd beneath the stormy Main.
What makes all this, but *Jupiter* the King,
At whose Command we perish, and we spring?
Then 'tis our best, since thus ordain'd to die,
To make a Vertue of Necessity.
Take what he gives, since to rebel is vain;
The Bad grows better, which we well sustain:
And cou'd we chuse the Time, and chuse aright,

'Tis best to die, our Honour at the height.
When we have done our Ancestors no Shame,
But serv'd our Friends, and well secur'd our Fame;
Then should we wish our happy Life to close,
And leave no more for Fortune to dispose:
So should we make our Death a glad Relief,
From future Shame, from Sickness, and from Grief:
Enjoying while we live the present Hour,
And dying in our Excellence, and Flow'r.

from The Cock and the Fox: or,
The Tale of the Nun's Priest

[Chanticleer]

And Rashers of sindg'd Bacon, on the Coals.
On Holy-Days, an Egg or two at most;
But her Ambition never reach'd to roast.
　　A Yard she had with Pales enclos'd about,
Some high, some low, and a dry Ditch without.
Within this Homestead, liv'd without a Peer,
For crowing loud, the noble Chanticleer:
So hight her Cock, whose singing did surpass
The merry Notes of Organs at the Mass.
More certain was the crowing of a Cock
To number Hours, than is an Abbey-clock;
And sooner than the Mattin-Bell was rung,
He clap'd his Wings upon his Roost, and sung:
For when Degrees fifteen ascended right,
By sure Instinct he knew 'twas One at Night.
High was his Comb, and Coral-red withal,
In dents embattel'd like a Castle-Wall;
His Bill was Raven-black, and shon like Jet,
Blue were his Legs, and Orient were his Feet:
White were his Nails, like Silver to behold,
His Body glitt'ring like the burnish'd Gold.
　　This gentle Cock for solace of his Life,
Six Misses had beside his lawful Wife;
Scandal that spares no King, tho' ne'er so good,
Says, they were all of his own Flesh and Blood:
His Sisters both by Sire, and Mother's side,
And sure their likeness show'd them near ally'd.
But make the worst, the Monarch did no more,
Than all the *Ptolomeys* had done before:
When Incest is for Int'rest of a Nation,

'Tis made no Sin by Holy Dispensation.
Some Lines have been maintain'd by this alone,
Which by their common Ugliness are known.
  But passing this as from our Tale apart,
Dame Partlet was the Soveraign of his Heart:
Ardent in Love, outragious in his Play,
He feather'd her a hundred times a Day:
And she that was not only passing fair,
But was withal discreet, and debonair,
Resolv'd the passive Doctrin to fulfil
Tho' loath: And let him work his wicked Will.
At Board and Bed was affable and kind,
According as their Marriage-Vow did bind,
And as the Churches Precept had enjoin'd.
Ev'n since she was a Sennight old, they say
Was chast, and humble to her dying Day,
Nor Chick nor Hen was known to disobey.
  By this her Husband's Heart she did obtain,
What cannot Beauty, join'd with Virtue, gain!
She was his only Joy, and he her Pride,
She, when he walk'd, went pecking by his side;
If spurning up the Ground, he sprung a Corn,
The Tribute in his Bill to her was born.
But oh! what Joy it was to hear him sing
In Summer, when the Day began to spring,
Stretching his Neck, and warbling in his Throat,
Solus cum Sola, then was all his Note.
For in the Days of Yore, the Birds of Parts
Were bred to Speak, and Sing, and learn the lib'ral Arts.

from The Art of Poetry

[Warning to Would-be Writers]

Rash Author, 'tis a vain presumptuous Crime
To undertake the Sacred Art of Rhyme;
If at thy Birth the Stars that rul'd thy Sence
Shone not with a Poetic Influence:
In thy strait Genius thou wilt still be bound,
Find *Phœbus* deaf, and *Pegasus* unsound.
   You then, that burn with the desire to try
The dangerous Course of charming Poetry;
Forbear in fruitless Verse to lose your time,
Or take for Genius the desire of Rhyme:
Fear the allurements of a specious Bait,
And well consider your own Force and Weight ...
There is a kind of Writer pleas'd with Sound,
Whose Fustian head with clouds is compass'd round,
No Reason can disperse 'em with its Light:
Learn then to Think, e're you pretend to Write.
As your Idea's clear, or else obscure,
Th' Expression follows perfect, or impure:
What we conceive, with ease we can express;
Words to the Notions flow with readiness.